The

Immigration

Invasion

**Wayne Lutton
and John Tanton**

with a Foreword by
Senator Eugene McCarthy

The Social Contract Press
Petoskey, Michigan

THE IMMIGRATION INVASION

Publishers' note: The text of this paperback
edition is available in a hardcover library
edition entitled *The Costs of Immigration*.

ISBN: 1-881780-01-5 (paperback)
ISBN: 1-881780-05-8 (hardcover)

First Printing: June 1994 (200,000 copies)

TABLE OF CONTENTS

DEDICATION

To the memory of the Founders of our Republic, who had the vision to write:

ARTICLE IV

Section 4. — The United States shall guarantee a republican form of government to every State in the Union and they **SHALL PROTECT EACH STATE AGAINST INVASION** and on application of the legislature, or the executive (when the legislature cannot be convened), against domestic violence.

The Constitution of the United States

FOREWORD
By Senator Eugene McCarthy

For the next generation, controlling immigration will be one of the main challenges facing all the industrial nations.

The driving force behind international migration is population growth in the Third World. The built-in momentum for the growth in human numbers is scarcely believable. Even if fertility dropped to replacement levels *today*, our ranks would still increase by 50 percent before they stopped growing. Based on persons *already born*, the work force in the Third World will see a net increase by 2010 of 800 million — a third more than all those currently employed in the developed world. Unemployment and under-employment rates in the less-developed countries are already 40 percent or more in many instances. The developed countries are cutting jobs left and right. Even the United States government is cutting its work force by 10 percent; more than 200,000 jobs! State and local governments are likewise freezing or reducing payrolls. The future will see more and more people seeking to fill a job base that already is not broad enough to provide decent employment for existing applicants.

John Tanton and Wayne Lutton understand what these facts and trends portend for the public. They have prepared a readable compendium on what these numbers mean for the United States and its immigration policy.

First, the book looks at the problems that the massive immigration of the last 30 years has generated. If you are looking for an encomium to immigrants, you won't find it here; that is not the authors' purpose. Tanton and Lutton do not deny that many immigrants are fine folks, but that story has been told in endless repetition. After all, *everything* about the human history of the United States — the good, the bad; the noble and ignoble — is attributable to immigration: we are all of immigrant stock at some point, including the Native Americans.

Rather, the authors contend that much of what is said about the behavior of recent immigrants is simply not true. They offer evidence that aliens are heavy users of welfare programs and are a burden to school districts. The notion that aliens "create jobs" for Americans is a myth, as the authors demonstrate: the few who do go into business for themselves, often hire only their own. Moreover, they do not "melt" as did earlier generations of immigrants.

Next, the authors present a helpful synopsis of U.S. immigration history, from which we can learn useful lessons.

Finally, they present an ethical framework for setting immigration policy, followed by their detailed and specific recommendations for changes. There is no waffling here.

When this kind of candid analysis has occurred in the past, many advocates of high immigration have tried to prevent public discussion by making personal attacks on the analysts. I hope the immigration debate has matured enough so that we can leave the *argumentum ad hominem* behind and stick to the issues. Critics of this book should present their own alternative suggestions for public critique and review. We shall see.

I recommend study of the immigration issue and of this thoughtful book to all Americans.

AUTHOR'S INTRODUCTION

Immigration is one of the most contentious issues confronting the American public today, as well as the citizens of other developed countries. Millions of people are on the move. Other millions in the receiving countries are asking what this massive human tide bodes for their future, where it will lead, and what can be done about it.

We have tried to answer these questions for the United States, reviewing a vast amount of material and filtering it through our long experience with this topic. The result is a fact-filled book divided into three parts:

I. **The Problem**. In the first five chapters we have tried to outline the main problems caused by the heavy immigration of the past 30 years.

II. **How We Got Into This Predicament**. The next four chapters summarize the history of U.S. immigration policy, consider the underlying forces that drive immigration, and draw attention to the special interest groups that use immigration to push their own agendas.

III. **The Solutions**. The final three chapters lay out the ethical basis for setting immigration policy, then give suggestions for what **you** can do.

One of our goals for this book is wide distribution. Toward that end, we have decided to publish it in an inexpensive paperback version, priced low enough so that we hope you will want to buy additional copies to distribute among your friends and associates. A hard cover version is also available.

This book has been two years in the making. New information kept coming in, requiring revisions. The topic now touches on so many aspects of American life that it has required a great deal of editing to balance the presentation and keep it to a manageable size. As with any joint effort, this was a division of labor. Chapters 1-2, 4, and 6-8 were written by Wayne Lutton, while John Tanton wrote Chapters 3, 5, and 9-12.

We had valuable help and criticism from Gerda Bikales, former executive director of U.S. ENGLISH, and now head of E Pluribus Unum; Robert Kyser, managing editor of *The Social Contract*; Roy Beck, Washington (D.C.) editor of *The Social Contract*; and from many other people active on the immigration issue, both inside and outside of government. We thank them all, as we do Niki Calloway, Dorothy Koury and Peggy Raddatz of *The Social Contract* staff for processing this manuscript through many versions. We, of course, accept the responsibility for the way in which the words all came together at the end.

Current plans call for producing a 20-minute video based on this book and periodically updating the text. Toward this end, the authors welcome your comments and suggestions.

Wayne Lutton   John Tanton

PART ONE: THE PROBLEM

CHAPTER ONE
HEALTH AND WELFARE COSTS
FOR IMMIGRANTS

At one time, facts about the effects of immigrants on our social welfare system were hard to come by, but now we have an impressive body of knowledge on these costs. In summary: immigrants who have come to the United States since 1965 are generally less well-educated and have fewer job skills and poorer language abilities than immigrants of earlier eras. It is hardly surprising to discover that these newer immigrants are more likely to use welfare than their predecessors.

The United States has become a "welfare magnet" to people around the world. Benefits granted by federal, state, and local agencies are typically far higher than the annual income in many countries of origin. [See Table 1-1]

Immigrant Welfare Use Increasing

Economists George Borjas of the University of California-San Diego, and Stephen Trejo of the University of California-Santa Barbara, in their study, *Immigrant Participation in the Welfare System,* confirm the validity of the "widespread perception that unskilled immigrants are particularly prone to enter the welfare system, and that the entry of large numbers of these immigrants in the past two decades has increased taxpayer expenditures of income transfer programs." Data from the 1970, 1980, and 1990 Censuses indicate that immigrant welfare dependency rates have been rising steadily since the onset of the 1965 immigration revisions and have become significantly higher — both in absolute terms and relative to native-born American citizens.[1]

Table 1
ANNUAL PER CAPITA INCOME
MAJOR SENDING COUNTRIES
(In U.S. Dollars)

Country	Income	Country	Income
Mexico	2165	Guyana	420
El Salvador	1020	Mainland China	320
Guatemala	1250	Vietnam	215
Colombia	1110	Laos	150
Peru	880	Cambodia	130
Nicaragua	470	Thailand	1160
Honduras	890	Korea	4600
Ecuador	935	Pakistan	409
Philippines	625	India	400
Cuba	2000	Bangladesh	180
Jamaica	1100	Iran	1800
Haiti	380	Nigeria	270
Dominican Rep.	790	Poland	4565

(Source: *Information Please Almanac, Atlas and Yearbook*, 1992, Boston: Houghton Mifflin Co.)

Professors Borjas and Trejo find that welfare use increases with the immigrant's age more quickly than it does among native-born Americans. By law, immigrants are subject to deportation if they become a "public charge" during their first three years of residency in the U.S. While this provision is almost never enforced, the possibility may discourage some recent immigrants from applying for aid. Borjas and Trejo also discovered that "the process of assimilation leads immigrants into welfare rather than out of it. [Immigrant] assimilation involves the accumulation of information not only about labor market opportunities, but also about alternative opportunities available through the welfare system."

Research conducted by Lief Jensen supports the conclusions reached by Borjas and Trejo. Writing in *International Migration Review* (Spring 1988), Professor Jensen noted that foreign-born residents of the United States were 56 percent more likely than native-born Americans to be living in poverty, 25 percent more likely to receive public aid, and to have an average per capita income from public assistance 13.6 percent higher than natives.

Welfare participation rates differ among immigrants. Those coming from less-developed countries and possessing skills that do not meet the requirements of a high-tech economy are much more likely to use welfare than are skilled immigrants from industrialized nations. The most recent census figures indicate that 29.3 percent of Vietnamese immigrants were on welfare, 25.8 percent of those from the Dominican Republic, 18 percent from Cuba, 12.4 percent from Mexico, all the way down to 4 percent from Denmark and 3.9 percent from Switzerland.

The traditional American work ethic placed a stigma on taking welfare. Recent immigrants are less apt to regard this as a disgrace. For instance, among the Chinese, who are often portrayed as the "Model Minority," it is " viewed as a normal benefit of immigration, whose use is actually encouraged, like a library card," Professor Norman Matloff of the University of California at Davis notes. Chinese seniors, who enter by way of family reunification provisions of current U.S. immigration statutes, frequently go on welfare as soon as the three-year waiting period expires. (In Canada, sponsoring children are financially responsible for their parents for 10 years). According to the 1990 Census, among Chinese seniors in California who came to the U.S. since 1980, 55 percent were on welfare, in contrast to 9 percent of native-born seniors. Many elderly Chinese are actually quite well off. But they have discovered that they can qualify for special welfare benefits by transferring many of their assets to their children. "A common viewpoint" among Chinese, Professor Matloff points out, is *"mh hou sit dai —* 'do not miss this good opportunity.'"[2]

Programs Used by Aliens

Immigrants are participating in more than fifteen major federally- and state-financed services. [See Table 1-2.] The largest expense category is public education, kindergarten

---

Table 2
MAJOR FEDERAL AND STATE
BENEFIT PROGRAMS
USED BY IMMIGRANTS

Aid to Families with Dependent Children
Supplemental Security Income (SSI)
General Assistance
Housing and Urban Development (HUD)
     Community Development Grants
Foster care, adoption assistance,
     and child welfare
Medicaid, emergency services and
     services for pregnant women
State and local medical care
School lunch and breakfast programs
Headstart
Job Training Partnership Act
Title IV for Higher Education
Block grants for social services
Adult Education Grants
Women, Infants and Children (WIC)
     and other child nutrition
Home Energy Assistance

(Source: Congressional Research Service
of the Library of Congress)

through high school. Thanks to a 1982 decision by the U.S. Supreme Court (*Plyler v. Doe*), taxpayers are required to provide free education to the children of illegal aliens.

Uncompensated medical care provided to illegal aliens at publicly supported hospitals follows education as the most costly burden to U.S. taxpayers. The average cost to taxpayers is $4700 *per admission*.[3]

Another program is the Earned-Income Tax Credit (EITC). This novel provision of our tax laws, adopted during the Nixon Administration, actually sends a check (rather than charging taxes) to persons who meet certain low income and dependency standards. Remarkably, nowhere in the IRS code does it state one must be a citizen or legal resident alien to apply for this benefit.

The authors are in possession of a copy of an income tax return filed by an illegal alien in Colorado. He received a full refund of his state and federal income taxes, obtained a tax credit against his food sales tax — and then got a check for $500 from the federal government! As of 1994, the maximum benefit available has been increased to $2,364, with further increases already scheduled for future years.

We have no idea how many aliens are taking advantage of this program. James Brovard reports that the EITC program is the "fastest growing, and most fraud prone welfare program... Between 30% and 40% of EITC benefits are given in violation of federal tax law" ("Clinton's Biggest Welfare Fraud," *Wall Street Journal*, May 10, 1994).

Immigration Increases the Cost of Government

Important cost elements that cannot be accurately estimated — but are no less real — are those for general services used by all persons residing in an area, regardless of their citizenship, such as police and fire protection, the courts, parks and other public facilities, transportation, and environmental protection. The costs of all of these services rise as population grows ... and immigration increases population.

Since 1970, U.S. immigration policies are responsible for an increase in our numbers of more than 27 million. Immigrants — and their children, because of high fertility rates — account for more than half of U.S. population growth since 1970. They are likely to contribute two-thirds of the anticipated increase through the remainder of the 1990s.[4]

American baby boomers are having small families, but large-scale immigration has doubled U.S. population growth over what it would have been without immigration. Thus, a significant part of the rising costs of public services can fairly be attributed to immigration.

The Role of the Courts

Over the past decade the courts have acted to extend welfare eligibility to illegal aliens. It seems odd that people who have broken federal laws and are not legal residents of the United States are nonetheless entitled to a host of benefits at taxpayers' expense. There is little doubt that the expansion of aliens' "rights" to include welfare acts as a magnet to attract even more immigrants, both legal and illegal.

A milestone in the continuing controversy over entitlements received by illegal aliens was the 1982 U.S. Supreme Court decision, *Plyler v. Doe*, which overturned a Texas law that denied school districts' funds for the education of children who are themselves illegal aliens. The Texas law gave districts the option of denying them admission or of charging tuition.

In their 5-4 decision, the Supreme Court majority declared this sensible law unconstitutional on the basis that no state may "deny to any person within its jurisdiction the equal protection of the laws." This, is paradoxical, for the Court has upheld the right of particular states to charge residents of other states higher "non-resident" tuition at public schools. In this case, the Court ruled that children who are residing in the country illegally have a right to free education paid for by the citizens of any state where they happen to be living. The average per-pupil cost in U.S. public schools is currently $4,800 annually, thus the total cost to taxpayers for educating the illegal alien children runs into billions of dollars. This figure does not include the extra costs for the bilingual education programs in which many of these students are enrolled. Along our southern border, many students commute daily from their homes in Mexico to attend school in the U.S., even though Plyler only applies to illegal aliens resident in this country. Not surprisingly, border school districts are among the poorest in the U.S.

A number of state courts have delivered rulings extending welfare benefits to illegal aliens. They have based their decisions on the curious legal concept of "Permanent Resident Alien Under Color of Law" (PRUCOL). This doctrine treats illegal aliens as *lawfully present* and thus fully entitled to all public aid, unless the individual alien has been served with a formal deportation order by the INS. An example of how this applies in practice is a 1984 California Court of Appeals ruling that extended medical benefits to illegals who are not undergoing federal deportation proceedings. Since that ruling, California taxpayers have been hit with hundreds of millions of dollars in unreimbursed medical expenses incurred by illegal aliens. If the employers of illegal aliens had to absorb these costs, they would have second thoughts about how profitable it is to hire them.

Similarly, in 1984, the Arizona State Supreme Court ruled that counties should reimburse hospitals for treating "resident" illegal aliens. Justice Stanley Feldman, writing for the majority, averred that illegal aliens establish residency in Arizona just by living in a county permanently, provided they do not seek a permanent home elsewhere. As *de facto* county residents, they are entitled to health and other taxpayer-financed welfare benefits.

The state of Illinois tried to remove illegal aliens from its welfare rolls by asking food stamp applicants about their immigrant status. But after the Mexican-American Legal Defense and Education Fund (MALDEF) filed a lawsuit challenging this directive of the Illinois Department of Public Aid, the U.S. District Court for the Northern District of Illinois ordered the Agency to stop questioning applicants about their nationality.

A Federal District judge in Brooklyn, New York, ruled in 1986 that illegal aliens living in New York State could not be denied Medicaid assistance. In response to a suit filed on behalf of nine "non-legal permanent resident aliens" by Washington Square Legal Services, Judge Charles Sifton declared that the federal statute creating Medicaid contained "no express restrictions on alien eligibility" and that federal authorities had thus acted improperly when they forbad Medicaid for illegal aliens. In his decision, Judge Sifton said that those "who are colloquially referred to as 'illegal aliens'" were, more accurately, people who had established permanent residence in this country but who had not yet been granted legal permanent resident status. Thus, through a series of decisions, illegal aliens have been granted "squatters' rights" to the American welfare system.

Sanctuary: Cities and States Extend Benefits to Aliens

Costs incurred by aliens are borne most heavily by state and local governments. The U.S. Congress has opened our borders to millions of people from around the globe, while making the states and cities where aliens settle responsible for bearing most of the costs incurred by these newcomers. State and municipal officials complain — correctly — that they are now being overwhelmed by escalating costs associated with the large-scale immigration of poor and unskilled people. And since immigration is a *federal* issue, they argue, it should be dealt with at that level.

But while they bemoan the costs incurred by the current wave of immigrants, only a few of them are now lobbying in Washington, D.C., for reducing the immigrant flow. On the contrary, throughout the 1980s, many states and municipalities declared themselves "sanctuaries" for aliens and have openly refused to cooperate with the INS in its efforts to apprehend illegal aliens or bar them from public services. Too often, they have offered programs that have tended to encourage aliens to move to their jurisdictions.

Under pressure from ethnic lobbyists, in late 1983, the Los Angeles County Department of Public and Social Services announced that they would refuse to forward to the INS the names of illegal aliens applying for welfare.

In February, 1984, California Governor George Deukmejian ordered the state's Employment Development Department not to implement directives that required non-citizens to provide proof that they were legally entitled to work before they could receive payments. This would have made it more difficult for illegal aliens to get unemployment insurance.

The city of San Jose, California, in May, 1984, declared that it would refuse to cooperate with the INS in weekly sweeps for aliens working illegally in Silicon Valley. Even though these on-site raids opened up jobs for American citizens, San Jose officials charged that the INS was "discriminatory, inhumane, and callous." The San Jose City Council voted 9-2 in favor of a resolution calling for the municipal police, "to the extent legally possible," to withhold any assistance to the INS in searches for illegal aliens employed locally.

In November, 1990, the Los Angeles City Council voted

in favor of a set of policy guidelines that placed further restrictions on Los Angeles Police Department (LAPD) cooperation with federal immigration authorities. As early as 1979, the LAPD, under Special Order 40, was prohibited from contacting the INS when they arrested an illegal alien, unless the alien was guilty of drug charges or a felony. The 1990 City Council action reaffirmed the intent of Special Order 40, and barred the Los Angeles police officers from arresting suspected illegal aliens.

Of those arrested during the Los Angeles riots of May, 1992, many were illegal aliens. When the LAPD handed over some of the alien rioters to the INS, who promised to quickly deport them, immigrant rights activists protested that this was in direct contravention of city policy not to turn over people to the INS. LAPD spokesman Lt. John Dunkin acknowledged that, "This was a departure from our normal policy, but this was not a normal situation."

Other states and municipalities have followed California's lead. In March, 1985, the city of Madison, Wisconsin, barred its police and other employees from cooperating with the INS. The city of Chicago quickly issued similar directives to its officials. The Cambridge (Massachusetts) City Council voted in April, 1985, to cease cooperating with the INS and extended educational and health services to illegal aliens.

New York City mayor Edward Koch issued an executive order prohibiting city agencies from barring illegal aliens from signing up for welfare benefits. Municipal officials could be fired if they attempted to discourage illegal aliens from obtaining taxpayer-provided services. Illegal immigrants who can prove that they have lived in the city for more than two years are even entitled to financial benefits denied to American citizens from out of town. A flier signed by Koch and distributed by the Mayor's Office of Immigrant Affairs in May, 1988, declared, "Immigrant New Yorkers: It is Your City

Too! Documented or undocumented, you are entitled to many City services." ... Illegal aliens were assured that "It is the City's policy not to report you to immigration authorities! ... I urge you to make use of them [city welfare and education benefits] so you and your family can have the best possible life." Mayor Koch went on to emphasize that, "many of these services are free." It is no surprise that New York, a city perpetually on the brink of bankruptcy, has become a destination of preference for hundreds of thousands of illegal aliens.

Washington, D.C. mayor Marion Barry, in 1984, ordered municipal agencies not to check the legal status of people applying for city services. As word spread that the nation's capital had become a "sanctuary," illegal aliens flooded into the city.

On May 6 and 7, 1991, Central American immigrants, many of them illegals from El Salvador, engaged in two nights of rioting in our nation's capital. The mayhem followed the shooting, by a black police officer, of a Salvadoran, Daniel Gomez, during his arrest for drinking in public. During the second night of violence, black and white hoodlums joined the Salvadorans in rioting and looting. Mayor Sharon Kelly quickly announced that INS agents would not be permitted to check the identifications of arrested rioters.

After what passes for order in Washington, D.C. was restored, leaders of Washington's immigrant community demanded more Spanish-speaking police officers, better jobs and job-training programs, and more recreational facilities in their neighborhoods.

Extending welfare benefits to illegal aliens is a practice that is no longer limited to state and local officials. In 1990, the city of Costa Mesa, California, tried to reserve federally subsidized public housing for U.S. citizens and legal immigrants. But the Bush Administration's Secretary of Housing and Urban Development (HUD), Jack Kemp, ruled that, "HUD's community development programs do not require citizenship or lawful resident alien status for eligibility." Kemp went on to remark that, in his opinion, "it would be discriminatory and counterproductive" to prohibit illegal aliens from living in public housing projects. He feared that if Costa Mesa and other cities were allowed to reserve public housing for legal residents this would have an "inflammatory impact in communities that we do not want in America."[5] The Clinton Administration has continued Kemp's policies.

The 1994 California Earthquake

In the wake of the earthquake which rocked California in early January of this year, federal and state relief agencies went out of their way to provide home loans and other long-term aid for illegal aliens living in the state. The Justice Department quickly issued a directive through the Public Affairs Department of the Los Angeles District Office of the INS, stating:

INS will not have any role in identifying individuals applying for assistance from governmental agencies during this emergency period.

INS will not request any information from other governmental agencies which have requested confidentiality by law.[6]

Illegal aliens were encouraged to take all the benefits that state and federal taxpayers were underwriting. The Federal Emergency Management Agency (FEMA) handed out untold numbers of $2000 checks, requiring recipients only that they provide some proof of residency, such as a rent or utility receipt, if they did not have Social Security numbers. Other FEMA loans were made available to illegals to help pay for "crisis counseling," temporary housing for up to 18 months, and rebuilding costs for homeowners.

A flier widely distributed by FEMA, printed in English and Spanish, read:

CAN I RECEIVE ASSISTANCE IF I AM NOT A LEGAL RESIDENT OF THE UNITED STATES?
YES

• *It is not obligatory to be a legal resident of the United States in order to ask for and receive disaster assistance. It is possible to receive help even if you do not have documentation. FEMA does not ask questions about your legal status when you are in this country.*

• *All information is confidential and is not given to the Immigration and Naturalization Service (INS), nor to the IRS. For more information on these programs, call 1-800-525-0321.*

• *Disaster assistance is a coordinated effort between the Office of Emergency Services (OES) and FEMA.*

• *Disaster assistance is available to everyone, regardless of race, color, sex, religion, nationality or wealth status. Anyone who feels they have been discriminated against should call 1-800-525-0321.*

The Border Patrol reports that after the earthquake there was a rush across the border to try to take advantage of this bonanza.

Given this scandalous record of failing to speak out for a controlled immigration policy, and then extending benefits to those here illegally, perhaps state and local governments have only themselves to blame for this portion of their financial plight.

States Are Paying the Price

The settlement of hundreds of thousands of new immigrants is costing taxpayers across the country hundreds of millions of dollars a year. States and cities where aliens concentrate are especially hard hit:

California

By 1993, California faced a $14 billion state budget deficit as the costs of education, medical care, welfare, and crime escalated. Governor Pete Wilson has pointed out that each category has been significantly inflated by the heavy flow of immigrants — both legal and illegal — into the state. Speaking of the state's recent immigrants, Wilson said, "We have consumers of expensive services, and they continue to grow. ... there is a limit to our ability to absorb immigrant populations."[7]

Figures compiled by California's Department of Finance show that the state has become a magnet for aliens:

- One-third of all refugees admitted by the U.S. settle in California. Of all refugees, 90 percent begin receiving public aid within the first four months of their residency.

- An estimated 200,000 refugees who originally went to other states resettled in California during the 1980s. (Incidentally, there is no constitutional way to require immigrants to live in specified areas — a strategy which might have helped spread this burden.)

- Of all the legal immigrants admitted in 1992, over one-third settled in California, continuing a pattern that started in the 1980s.

Governor Wilson was correct to cite immigration as a major contributor to the state's fiscal crisis. The following is a sample of the costs associated with large-scale immigration to the state:

- Medical services for pregnancy and emergency care for illegal aliens cost the state and federally funded MediCal program an estimated $1 billion in 1993.

- Overall, the state's spending on health care for illegal immigrants has increased 5-fold over the past five years.

- Illegal alien children comprise almost 7 percent of the state's total school population. Their education is costing Californians nearly $2 billion a year.

Under current law, most alien children — whether their parents are here legally or illegally — must be taught in their native language in programs that cost, on average, $6600 per student annually, versus $4000 per student per year to educate children who are fluent in English. Nearly 100 languages are now spoken in California schools and bilingual teachers receive bonuses of up to $5000.

California's schools used to rank among the nation's very finest, but now they are at the bottom of schools in industrial states. *Newsweek*, May 4, 1992, reported, "The student population is exploding — fueled by a wave of mostly poor, mostly non-English-speaking immigrants — many of them illegal. The situation has grown so desperate ... that California would have to build a new 600-student school *every day for five years* just to maintain its sorry status quo." By the year 2000, the state's student population is expected to rise 46 percent, to nearly 7 million.

As Ted Hilton, director of the San Diego-based Coalition for Immigration Law Enforcement, observed, "Without this [additional educational] financial burden, California could substantially reduce its current budget deficit ... and improve the quality of education of all its lawful residents — including impoverished African-Americans and other minorities, and also legal immigrants — if we did not have to educate unlawful residents as well."

According to Michael Antonovich, chairman of the Los Angeles County Board of Supervisors, Los Angeles County and its county and city school districts are currently paying an estimated $1.16 billion every year for services provided to illegal aliens. This burden substantially contributed to the Los Angeles Unified School District's 1991 $274 million deficit.

Richard Dixon, Chief Administrative Officer for Los Angeles County, issued a report on April 22, 1991, outlining the impact that illegal immigration is having in their jurisdiction. Said Dixon, "The Federal government's inability to control our nation's borders has resulted in an ever-growing impact on the County; the estimated net cost to the County of services provided to undocumented aliens has grown from $207.2 million in 1989-90 to $276.2 million in 1990-91."

Among the highest-cost categories are Aid to Families with Dependent Children (AFDC) payments for the children born in the U.S. to illegal alien parents. Unlike many other countries, the U.S. grants immediate citizenship to anyone who happens to be born here. Citizen-children of illegal aliens numbered 97,665 (in Los Angeles County alone) by February, 1991. Total AFDC payments to these new citizen-children increased from $103.9 million in 1988-89 to $249.1 million in 1990-91. "A major concern is that total AFDC payments to these children and their families could easily reach $1 billion a year by the end of the decade, even if illegal immigration levels off. ... The number of citizen-children can be expected to grow due to the high birthrate of the undocumented alien population who are disproportionately of child-bearing age," Dixon's report noted.

During 1990-91, nearly 63 percent of the 57,366 births in Los Angeles County-funded hospitals were to mothers who are illegal aliens, an increase of 40 percent from 1988-89. In 1992, children born to illegal immigrants accounted for more than 65 percent of all such births.

Despite increased state and federal funding, the county has been forced to assume an enormous burden for unreimbursed health care costs for illegal aliens, as the following table indicates:

LOS ANGELES COUNTY
UNREIMBURSED HEALTH CARE COSTS
FOR ILLEGAL ALIENS
1983-1989

1983-84:	$99.8 million
1984-85:	$114.9 million
1985-86:	$123.7 million
1986-87:	$125.8 million
1987-88:	$141.6 million
1988-89:	$163.0 million

*SOURCE: County of Los Angeles
Department of Health Services*

Los Angeles County's Board of Supervisors is to be commended for its interest in trying to determine just how much immigration is costing their taxpayers. In San Diego County, an August 1992 report by the state Auditor General's Office concluded that the net cost of undocumented immigrants in that county was $146 million a year. Nine percent of the population of San Diego county is here illegally, including 25,000 children. AFDC funds totalling $11 million assist births to undocumented women. It has been *conservatively* estimated by the state Auditor that the net costs of services for the undocumented in San Diego County alone are enough to cover the 1991-92 budget deficits of the San Diego county and all the eighteen cities of the region.

A follow-up study conducted by San Diego State

University for the county found that the costs of providing services to illegal aliens in San Diego increased by nearly $100 million in little more than a year. The report, issued in October, 1993, concluded that the net cost of illegal immigration in that one county climbed to $244 million a year.

At the Chula Vista welfare office near the border, the parking lot is often full of cars with Baja [Mexico] license plates. Rules concerning a client's "privacy" have interfered with efforts to delete illegal aliens from the welfare rolls, despite the fact that illegal aliens arrested by the Border Patrol have been found carrying food stamps and California welfare checks.

Donald Huddle, of Rice University, has prepared the most comprehensive study on what immigration is costing California. He found that, overall, immigration cost Californians $18.1 billion in 1992 alone. Of this, only a quarter was incurred by illegal aliens. Legal and legalized immigrants were responsible for nearly three-quarters of the total, including education, Medi-Cal, county health/social services, and AFDC.[8] Dr. Huddle concludes that, based on Census Bureau projections and other sources, the net cost of immigration for California taxpayers will rise throughout the rest of the 1990s, averaging $26.5 billion per year.

Florida

Like California, Florida has been a major preferred destination for aliens from around the world. Approximately one million refugees arrived in Florida during the 1980s, and many remain there.

Immigration has had a significant impact on the state's budget, its tax load, social services, job market, natural resources, and infrastructure. Assistance to Cubans and Haitians who entered in the 1980s has cost Florida taxpayers hundreds of millions of dollars. Governor Lawton Chiles says Florida spends over $1 billion annually on illegal aliens and refugees.[9]

According to the Florida Department of Health and Rehabilitation Services, welfare payments to aliens from Central America who have applied for "refugee" status cost taxpayers $47 million a year. At the beginning of the 1992 legislative session, the chairwoman of the House Appropriations Subcommittee for Health and Rehabilitative Services, State Representative Elaine Gordon (D-North Miami), introduced legislation that would have barred some asylum applicants from receiving welfare. This seemingly sensible measure would have saved Florida taxpayers $23 million or more annually, but in early March the Florida Senate rejected her bill, after it had passed the House.

In a March 4, 1992, letter to then President Bush, Dade County (Greater Miami) Public Schools Superintendent Octavio Visiedo pointed out that 26 percent of their students were born outside of the United States. An average of 1200 foreign-born students enrolled in Miami-area schools each month during the 36-month period ending January, 1992. During 1991-92, the operating expenditure per student came to $4,336. The immediate cost of providing classroom space for the students — who hail from 118 foreign countries — is $136 million, with a long-range construction cost estimated to be $665 million. This does not include operation and maintenance.

Texas

Texas receives the third largest number of immigrants. Immigration has an impact on every aspect of Texas life — education, social service costs, and job displacement.

During the 1980s, 594,628 legal immigrants settled in Texas, and 174,132 more arrived in 1990. The number of illegal aliens living in the state is not known. However, the Border Patrol apprehended 418,705 persons trying to enter Texas surreptitiously from Mexico in 1991. Since the Border Patrol estimates that for every illegal alien arrested, two to three enter undetected, a *low* estimate for illegals entering through Texas in 1991 would be one million or more. How many eventually return home is also not known — the INS stopped keeping records on those leaving the country in 1957.

The cost to Texas taxpayers of educating the children of illegal aliens is heavy and rising. A 1990 Texas survey determined that illegal aliens were costing schools in the Texas border area as much as $26 million.

Governor Ann Richards' office estimates that the state spends $166 million each year for services provided to an estimated 550,000 illegal aliens. Said Leticia Vasquez, an aide to Governor Richards, "We do have a problem. We see it in schools, public hospitals, corrections, higher education, AFDC [the largest component of welfare]."

New York

New York ranks fourth among immigrant-receiving states. Most immigrants reside in New York City, 28 percent of whose residents are foreign-born. Since the early 1980s, New York has also been among the states offering the most enticing package of social service benefits to aliens, legal and illegal alike. Education, health care, and other costs are high, and the total cost to taxpayers for this generosity is estimated to total at least $5.6 billion annually.[10]

Over the past three years, New York City public schools have enrolled 120,000 additional children from 167 countries, speaking 185 languages and dialects. Often illiterate in their native languages, New York City has tried to fill vacancies for bilingual instructors, often imported for this purpose, while cutting back on the number of regular teachers. The additional annual cost for bilingual instruction is $687 per student. As *The Christian Science Monitor* reported in its issue of May 18, 1992, "After Spanish, the most commonly spoken languages at the schools are Chinese, Urdu, and Bengali. Every notice is sent home in Spanish and English, even report cards.

Translators are present at all parent-teacher conferences." Immigrant-language programs are costing New York City taxpayers $130.6 million every year.

Classroom space is very short. City officials estimate that it will cost $4.3 billion to build new schools and renovate existing structures to accommodate the burgeoning student population. Then, of course, these must be maintained and operated at additional cost.

Vast pools of cheap immigrant labor have driven down wage rates in the New York metropolitan area. Jobs that once paid a salary that allowed an individual to support a family no longer do so. High rates of illegal immigration are redefining the underclass.

Sweatshop industries are booming. Chinatown is a center for such enterprises which specialize in the manufacture of clothing, sporting goods, and toys. Pay seldom averages more than $150 for 60-hour work weeks and living conditions are grim. In April of 1991, housing authorities discovered that a warehouse in lower Manhattan had been divided into dozens of 6-by-9-foot windowless cubicles, smaller than jail cells. Often shared by two or three occupants, each rented out for $300 a month. The residents all shared one toilet, one shower head, and an encrusted gas stove for cooking. The owner was listed as Wing Tat Realty.

Many "refugees" sponsored by churches and other service agencies have found that the state's welfare benefits exceed wages they might earn, so they do not even bother to look for work. *The Buffalo News*, September 8, 1991, reported that one Tonawanda, New York church that sponsored more than 300 Ukrainians over the previous two years decided not to bring in any more. "It was sad to see what the welfare program here did to the people we sponsored," said the Reverend Mark Hill. Church members were chagrined to learn that welfare provides much more money for families than entry-level jobs.

According to Elsa Nachreiner, who works with the refugees, the newcomers' view is: "Why should we work at jobs which do not pay much? We are getting everything we need from welfare."

State lawmakers have been debating the idea of installing an automatic fingerprint-identification system designed to ferret out welfare abusers. Applicants would be fingerprinted and an optical image of their prints sent to a central computer for matching against the fingerprints of everyone on the general welfare rolls. This system would help prevent the fraud of duplicate claims. Los Angeles instituted this system in April, 1992. New York State Senator Tarky Lombardi, Jr., chair of the State Senate Finance Committee, estimates that such a system could save around $75 million annually. An aide to Senator Lombardi, Robert Penna, noted that "welfare fraud is a cottage industry in New York." In general, "all you have to do is have a pulse and you qualify."

If enacted nationwide, such a system could save taxpayers more than $25 billion a year.

Some communities in New York State are considering rescinding the welcome for "refugees" they extended in the 1980s. The Suffolk County Legislature, which proclaimed itself a "refugee sanctuary" in 1986, is considering repealing a measure promising illegal aliens that they will not be reported to the INS if they apply for welfare. Said county representative, Rose Caracappa, who supports repeal of their Illegal Immigrants Access Act, "The county is dying right now. With the recession going on and the increase in health and social services rolls, we do not have the caseworkers to handle the influx of cases coming in. I feel that as a legislator it is my responsibility to address the needs of the legal residents, before we address the needs of the illegals."

David Grunblatt, chairman of the New York County Lawyer's Association Immigration Committee, fears that if

Suffolk County repeals its welcome for aliens, other parts of the state will do likewise. "It is one of those cases where the first one to jump in the hot water cools it for everyone else," Grunblatt remarked.[11]

Massachusetts

Massachusetts ranks seventh in the U.S. as an immigrant-receiving state and fifth in refugee arrivals. Most state and local government agencies and service providers are not required to collect data that could be used to determine accurately the impact of immigration in the Bay State.

It is known that approximately 245,000 legal immigrants, refugees, and illegal aliens settled in Massachusetts during the 1980s — 110,000 of whom are illegal aliens, according to that state's Office for Refugees and Immigrants.

One-fourth of Lowell's 100,000 residents are from Southeast Asia. At the opening of the school year in 1989, over 10 percent of the state's public school students spoke a primary language other than English. The unemployment rate of Southeast Asian "refugees" in Worcester was 50 percent or higher.

According to the latest census, from 1980 to 1990, the Hispanic component of Massachusetts's population more than doubled, from 141,000 to 288,000. The state's Asian population almost tripled, from 49,000 to 143,000, with the bulk of the increase attributable to immigration.

"Refugees" on Welfare

Nearly two decades after the end of the Vietnam War, Indochinese "refugees" are still pouring into the U.S. at the rate of 50,000 per year. Defenders of immigration have portrayed refugees as successful people, who often make better citizens than native-born Americans.

Welfare use by refugees in many areas has been heavy. In San Joaquin County, California, over 78 percent have been receiving public assistance, with 93 percent of the refugee welfare clients claiming AFDC. A United Way study found that the over one million Asian-Pacific aliens living in greater Los Angeles constitute "a community about to explode" that requires massive increases in social and health services. Gary Wong, United Way task force chairman, observed that, "Asians tend to suffer from the stereotype that they are the model minority — the scholars, good incomes, stable family life. This study has identified the other side to that."

Of all the refugees who have settled in California since 1976, around 53 percent are dependent on AFDC and other welfare programs. A 1992 Federal Health & Human Services study of Southeast Asian refugees who arrived after 1985, found 52 percent to be totally dependent on welfare and an additional 13 percent to be supplementing earned income with welfare benefits.[12]

Thousands of Laotians have relocated from California to Minnesota, Wisconsin, and other states in the interior. Some moved to be with families, living where welfare benefits also happened to be higher. John Petraborg, assistant commissioner of the Minnesota Human Services Department, fears that they will become a permanent welfare class: "We are having talks with leaders of the Hmong community to encourage the idea of self-sufficiency."

Refugees have quickly learned how to milk the "system" for all it is worth. The *Los Angeles Times*' Mark Arax reports:

> *Federal, state, and local officials, responding to reports of widespread welfare fraud among Southeast Asian refugees in California, are calling for stronger law enforcement and increased community education to combat the problem. ... New approaches are needed to deter a large number of refugees who are supplementing welfare benefits with thousands of dollars a year in unreported wages. ... The Los Angeles County*

Board of Supervisors will urge better education for refugees about their responsibilities as welfare recipients. Refugees say they can take in considerably more by combining welfare benefits, Medi-Cal, and unreported income [than by working]. [This has] helped create the highest welfare dependency rate in the nation for Asian refugees. ... Several welfare case workers who are Indochinese said that they frequently know when a Southeast Asian family is earning cash from an underground job. But almost always they choose not to investigate, citing cultural reasons and the difficulty of making a successful case against a family.

Jane Gross, in a special story published by *The New York Times*, December 29, 1991, profiled a Cambodian refugee family who have become "welfare migrants."

Say Vann, his wife, and six children, moved sight unseen from Pennsylvania, their initial American state of residence, to sunny California. "What the Vanns found here [in California] was just what they had hoped for, just what fellow Cambodian refugees promised," she reported. The Vanns have averaged $200 a month more in welfare payments than they received in Pennsylvania, their medical bills are paid for by Medi-Cal, and they obtain $170 a month in food stamps. The Vann family — including Mr. Vann — is being educated at taxpayers' expense. The senior Vann was a foreman in a sugar factory in Phnom Penh before coming to the U.S. But since arriving here eleven years ago, the family has collected welfare.

The Vanns are representative of the large, poor families who, Governor Wilson warns, are contributing to California's education and health-care crisis, and compounding the impact of the recession. Wilson predicts a fiscal "train wreck" for a state that has 12 percent of America's population and 26 percent of its welfare load, if costs are not curbed and dependent migrants are not discouraged from settling there.

Conclusions

Legal and illegal immigrants are increasingly a burden to the United States. In 1992, immigrants in the U.S. since 1970 cost U.S. taxpayers $42.5 billion net in public assistance in excess of the $20.2 billion they paid in taxes.

In addition, an estimated 2.07 million American workers were displaced in 1992 by immigrants at a net cost of $11.9 billion in public aid.

Future net costs for the 1993-2002 decade are projected at $668.5 billion, for an average of $67 billion per year — unless immigration laws and enforcement are changed.[13]

The granting of social benefits to recent immigrants, and even to people who have settled here illegally, while requiring of them few of the duties of citizenship, is undermining the very concept of nationhood. As Latin America specialist Daniel James observes, "The concept of community becomes hollow if outsiders can enter it in defiance of its laws and regulations, and swiftly gain entitlements to benefits. The very viability of the U.S. welfare system is threatened when resources for the neediest are diluted by the claims of outsiders, and taxpayers conclude that the number of potential claimants is not limited by national boundaries."[14]

CHAPTER TWO
LABOR MARKET IMPACT
SHOULD WE IMPORT MORE WORKERS?

The United States has been going through economic hard times. The official national unemployment rate in early 1994 stood at just under 7 percent. When "discouraged workers" (those who want to work but have lost just about all hope of obtaining employment) and those who are involuntarily working only part-time are added, the overall rate of unemployment and underemployment probably exceeds 15 percent, or double the official figure.

Yet, despite massive joblessness, the United States intentionally imports a million or more additional job seekers every year — while looking the other way as millions more come in illegally.

As previously noted, the 1990 Immigration Act increased legal immigration by nearly 40 percent. At the time it was being pushed through Congress, it was often described as a "jobs bill." That is because proponents claimed that the United States faced an impending shortage of workers.

Ben Wattenberg, of the American Enterprise Institute, asserted that the huge federal budget deficit could be eliminated if more immigrants were admitted.[1] University of Maryland Marketing Professor Julian Simon, a former senior fellow at the conservative Heritage Foundation and favorite of *The Wall Street Journal*, testified that:

> *Immigrants do not take jobs, they create jobs. ... My recommendation would be that we simply jump immigration visas to one million per year ... there is no*

change [in public policies] that could have even a
fraction of the economic benefit that we can get simply
by increasing the number of immigrants by 100
percent.[2]

The exact impact of immigration on employment patterns is debated by many people. But, during a time of high unemployment, we should certainly not add hundreds of thousands of job seekers to already saturated job markets.

Nevertheless, immigration advocates in Congress point to Simon's flawed arguments as "proof" that we can absorb ever growing numbers of immigrants.

Vernon Briggs, Professor of Industrial and Labor Relations at Cornell University, takes an opposing view. He recently pointed out that in the twelve years preceding the onset of the 1990-1992 recession, the U.S. labor force underwent a huge expansion — one-third larger than the combined growth of the other nine major industrial countries (outside of the former Soviet Union). "None of the nation's major international competitors are faced with comparable pressures to accommodate so many new job seekers," he points out.[3]

Legal immigrants, including relatives of previously admitted aliens, as well as amnestied aliens, have arrived in record numbers with almost no consideration for their possible impact on the U.S. economy.

Less than 5 percent of legally admitted immigrants are certified by the Department of Labor as possessing job skills and educational attainments actually needed by the economy. When illegal aliens are included, the percentage of immigrants entering our work force because of our need for their specific talents is minuscule.

The overwhelming majority of immigrants, both legal and illegal, who have arrived since the 1965 Immigration Act are from Third World countries. Many have less than five years of education and are illiterate in their native language, let alone in English.

They compete most directly with those Americans who themselves are experiencing high rates of unemployment — teenagers, women, and racial minorities (including Hispanic-Americans).

Far from contributing to our general economic well-being, massive immigration is hurting the employment prospects of many Americans.

Effects on Low-skilled Workers

The Center for Immigration Studies confirms that overall unemployment rates in the occupations where immigrants most often compete for work are well above the national average.[4]

Three-quarters of foreign-born job seekers concentrate in just seven states, five of which now have jobless rates above the national average.

Six cities that attract the most immigrants — Miami, Los Angeles, New York, San Diego, Anaheim, and Chicago — all have unemployment rates well above the national average, with New York, Los Angeles, and Anaheim exceeding the national rate by over 40 percent.[5]

Thirty-four metropolitan areas where immigrants settle in large numbers are on the Labor Department's list of "labor surplus" localities and can therefore qualify for federal procurement preferences, based on two or more years of unemployment 20 percent above the national average.

Conversely, the areas that have fared best during the recession, do not have large populations of recent immigrants. The states with the largest job gains during 1991 included Nebraska (4.1 percent payroll growth), Arkansas (3.3 percent), South Dakota (2.7 percent), Alaska (2.6 percent), Idaho (2.5 percent), and Utah (2.4 percent).

The presence of large numbers of recent immigrants in the U.S. work force has yet to spark a national reaction, and there have been few calls to repeal the increase in legal immigration provided for in the 1990 Immigration Act. This is probably due to the persistence of two commonly held, but mistaken, views about participation by aliens in the economy: **first**, that they are mostly employed as seasonal agricultural workers, and **second**, that they generally take jobs that Americans simply will not perform.

Despite the fact that they are working here illegally, a considerable body of research has been conducted over the years, which has revealed a great deal about the participation of aliens in the work force. The evidence shows that relatively few immigrants (perhaps 8 to 15 percent) are employed in seasonal agriculture; the vast majority are employed in sectors of the economy where millions of Americans compete for work, frequently holding good jobs that citizens would gladly fill.

In April, 1982, at a time when unemployment was at approximately current levels, the INS conducted "Operation Jobs," a major effort that led to the arrest of thousands of illegal aliens on the job. Eighty-two plants in nine metropolitan areas were raided.

In Chicago, illegals were discovered holding jobs that paid from $4.82 to nearly $17 an hour. In Denver, illegal aliens were found working at jobs paying over $12 an hour. At that time, the hourly minimum wage was $3.35. The average wage paid to illegals apprehended in San Francisco was $5.19 an hour — 55 percent over the minimum wage. Businesses where illegal aliens were removed from the work force were swamped with applications from job-seeking citizens.

Rice University economist Donald Huddle has conducted field studies of the employment of illegal aliens in Houston, during times of both economic growth and recession. He has found that illegals continue to find employment in commercial construction and other sectors of the economy where wages range from the minimum rate to $10 or more an hour. Professor Huddle observed that, "these wages debunk the commonly held notion that illegal aliens are taking only those jobs that Americans do not want because they are lowly paid."[6]

The number of illegals working in Texas is not known. A 1989 study conducted by Dr. Huddle suggested that 200,000 lived in the Houston area alone, holding jobs in construction, landscaping, and light manufacturing. He estimated that two out of every three of the jobs currently held by illegal aliens could be filled by Americans.

According to Huddle, during the recession of 1982-1983, approximately 3.5 million Americans were displaced in the labor force by illegal aliens. For every 100 illegal aliens who were employed, 65 U.S. workers were displaced or remained unemployed.

In 1984, an INS survey discovered that 25 percent of the employees in Silicon Valley were illegal aliens. As Harold Ezell, then INS western regional commissioner, observed, "These are jobs that belong to U.S. citizens and permanent residents."

That same year, Representative Fortney Stark (D-CA), disclosed that nearly 550,000 aliens were using "non-work" Social Security cards to obtain employment in the U.S. These documents are issued to visitors, such as students and tourists, to enable them to open bank accounts, make investments, and pursue other lawful activities for which such identification is required.

In past years, the Social Security Administration has compiled lists of the names, addresses, and employers of aliens working here illegally, but there has been little follow-up to remove them from the work force, owing in part to privacy rules that prohibit agencies from sharing information.

Professor Huddle has recently prepared two studies detailing the impact that immigrants, legal and illegal, are having on the U.S. work force.[7] He found that:

- Based on research by Professors Joseph Altonji and David Card, it is clear that the earnings of low-skilled American workers — black males, black or white females with not more than 12 years of education, and white males with less than 12 years of education are seriously depressed in areas where they compete in the job market with large numbers of immigrants. A 10 percent increase in the number of immigrants in a particular Standard Metropolitan Statistical Area, results in a 12 percent decline in weekly earnings, with black males' earnings reduced by almost 20 percent.

- Low-skilled American workers are hurt more by illegal immigrants than by legal immigrants. This is because illegals often work for lower wages than legal immigrants and citizens; they enjoy little legal protection from employers who exploit them; and they provide a major cost advantage to employers who hire large numbers of illegals, since employers frequently do not withhold federal and state income taxes, make Social Security contributions, or pay workers' compensation.

- Hundreds of thousands of Americans are being directly displaced from jobs by recent immigrants.

The Misery Index

Professor Huddle has created a "Misery Index" to measure the impact that growing numbers of immigrants are having on the employment of unskilled Americans. The misery index is defined as the measured negative changes in three labor force categories — the wage rate, the ratio of labor force participation to population, and the fraction of the past year worked. Declines in these measures mean less work and lower earnings and hence more misery for the unskilled native work force.

The 25 metropolitan areas with the largest numbers of recent immigrants also ranked highest on the Misery Index, with Miami, Florida, leading with an index of 24.7 percent, followed by Los Angeles, California, with 20.1 percent, Jersey City, New Jersey, with 15.5 percent and Houston, Texas, with 12.4 percent.

He concludes that, "immigration has substantial negative wage and employment effects. ... U.S. immigration policy has penalized U.S. minorities and unskilled workers. ... More legal immigration due to the 1990 Immigration Reform means higher displacement and wage depression for America's unskilled workers."

Aliens Recruit Aliens

A major factor in the displacement of Americans is that many jobs are simply not available to them.

In labor-intensive fields, growing numbers of employers have found it profitable to let aliens do the recruiting. As Professor Philip Martin of the University of California at Davis explains, all too frequently job openings are not advertised in newspapers or listed with state employment services. Instead, aliens recruit other aliens by word of mouth.

Over time, the work places become "colonized" by aliens to the degree that Americans are not welcome and would find themselves strangers if employed at these establishments. If aliens leave for other employment, or are expelled by government authorities, employers have been known to contract with "coyotes" to hire alien replacements. "The cross-border recruitment system," Martin points out, "provides illegal alien workers with a more sophisticated job search network than is available to many unemployed American workers."[8]

Proponents of increased immigration, notably Julian Simon, argue that, "immigrants not only take jobs, they create (some) jobs." True, but often as not, the new jobs benefit other aliens, not Americans.

Journalist Donatella Lorch describes how this process is transforming important sectors of the economy in the New York metropolitan area. Recent immigrants from the Indian subcontinent now operate about 40 percent of the city's gas stations (Koreans dominate this sector in Los Angeles); over 85 percent of the green-grocer stores are owned and operated by Koreans; Indians and Pakistanis now enjoy a virtual monopoly on newsstands and are now moving into the jewelry trade. Guyanese are a growing presence in drugstore operations and machinery repair. Jamaicans and Irish now compete for control of the child-care business, while Afghans are coming to dominate the fast-food chicken trade.

"Once a niche is found, it creates a snowball effect," she explains, "gathering in labor from that ethnic group and expanding exponentially. ... The common thread linking all immigrant work niches is the insider's edge on the profession."[9]

Elizabeth Bogan, in her book, *Immigration in New York*, writes that, thanks to the "ethnic hiring networks and the proliferation of immigrant-owned small businesses in the city [that] have cut off open market competition for jobs ... there are tens of thousands of jobs in New York City for which the native-born are not candidates."

In the Professions, Too

Even as thousands of white-collar professionals are being laid off across the nation, such firms as Grumman, Hughes, Northrop, Rockwell, Boeing, the Sundstand Corporation, and others have been importing workers on "temporary" visas.

Business Week described how Russian scientists, who came here as favored and subsidized refugees, are moving into the U.S. computer industry and are busy recruiting more citizens of the former Soviet Union now that travel restrictions have been eased.

At a time of substantial layoffs among American engineers and scientists, Russians are flocking to America "on long and short-term fellowships and work contracts to fill jobs everywhere from Cambridge, Massachusetts to Silicon Valley."

The *Business Week* article highlighted the career of Naum Staroselsky, winner of the U.S. Small Business Association's 1986 "Small Business Innovation Award," and the Midwest's "Entrepreneur of the Year" for 1990. A Ph.D. from Leningrad Polytechnic, his Iowa-based Compressor Controls Corporation is hiring more Russians, who work for a fraction of what American engineers with 10 to 15 years' experience should command.[10]

According to the National Science Foundation, about 35 percent of all engineers now working in the U.S. are foreign-born.

The hiring of aliens in skilled occupations is increasing. Employers often prefer to hire them because they will work for less than the American pay scale.

Aliens can legally work in the U.S. if their employer petitions the Labor Department and asserts that they are "persons of distinguished merit and ability," making them eligible for the so-called H-1B visas, and that they are filling a job for which no American citizens are available.

Immigration employment specialists tailor job descriptions to enable aliens to legally accept professional positions here. Often they are average people with very average levels of education, ability, and work habits, but are just willing to work for considerably lower salaries than their American counterparts.

To qualify for an H-1 visa, an alien need only have an undergraduate degree in the field, or two years of college and five years "experience," to be designated by the Labor Department as "a person of outstanding merit."

The following examples illustrate how the services of aliens are marketed to firms in the U.S.:

- In a letter introducing CHEMTECH International Services of Pasadena, California, Ronald LaValle, managing director for U.S. operations, pointed out that if a "cost-conscious" manager is looking for engineers, "we have available British engineers with excellent qualifications and experience levels, who are prepared to work here in the United States of America for as much as a 40 percent reduction in current United States salary levels."

- OMNI Personnel Services of San Jose, California sends Philippine contract workers to Canada, Britain, Italy, and Saudi Arabia. In a proposal to place Filipinos with U.S.-based companies, their director of contract workers noted that his clients are known for their hard work and command of the English language. "To top it all," he emphasizes, "hiring Filipino technical workers is more advantageous because it means an increase in profit for your company due to the sizeable reduction in their wages."

At the Universities

American higher education is fast becoming a lucrative field for foreign professionals. Universities frequently go overseas to recruit foreign students. Many colleges and universities are staffing their departments of mathematics, business, and engineering with legal aliens.   The practice is expanding to the liberal arts, propelled by "affirmative action" requirements for the hiring of favored "minorities." That they are foreign-born and have no claim on our system for redress of past grievances, apparently makes no difference to our legislators and the university administrators.

The Chronicle of Higher Education has run ads listing the services of the "Minority Faculty Registry," based at Southwestern University, Georgetown, Texas, which offers to help candidates specially favored as minorities find employment at colleges and universities across the country.

"Current visa status" is asked of applicants, who can be assisted to obtain authorization for legal employment. More than half the registrants (51 percent) were non-citizens.[11] In many instances, the aliens first came to the U.S. on student visas. Thanks to policies designed to help "minorities," they can remain here and take a place in the job line ahead of native-born Americans.

A number of schools have found that foreign-born "minority" professors do not relate well to native students. Stanford University recently began offering financial incentives to encourage the hiring of "minority" teachers who were born in the U.S. "We do value diversity," said Kathryn Gillam, assistant provost for faculty affairs, "[but] having somebody who is born in Zaire does not help [students] if they were brought up in Chicago."

Immigrants Rights lobbyists fear that Stanford's move may close off job opportunities for foreigners. "That is outrageous" said Robert Rubin, assistant director of the Lawyers Committee for Civil Rights in San Francisco. Jack Pemberton, an attorney with the U.S. Equal Employment Opportunity Commission, offered that, "This [trying to hire American citizens instead of aliens] is the strangest thing I have ever heard."[12]

According to *The Christian Science Monitor* (December 27, 1991), more than 50 percent of all faculty under the age of 36 in American universities today are foreign-born.

Over 300,000 of these special foreign entrants find employment here every year. "Non-immigrant workers" are supposed to work here only temporarily. However, their visas can be extended for up to six years. Meanwhile, many "temporary" workers manage to change their status and never go home.

During the past four years, over 100,000 companies have requested "special skills" papers to enable them to hire lower-paid foreign professionals — especially for civil engineers, computer programmers, and physical therapists. Paul Elmer, international human resources director at Motorola, Inc., defends the practice, claiming, "It is important to get new blood into the organization."[13]

Does Our Economy Need Immigrants?

The question that needs to be asked is this: "Does our economy really require large numbers of immigrants?"

Given the lower average education and skills of many recent immigrants, as shown by Professor George Borjas in his book, *Friends or Strangers: The Impact of Immigrants on the U.S. Economy*, plus the need to provide education and opportunities for our own citizens, the answer is a resounding, "No." Even Professor Julian Simon, in response to the question, "Is immigration really necessary to the economy?" admits, "We can live nicely without it."

As Benjamin Matta pointed out in *Labor Law Journal*, "The vast majority of the current immigrant supply is substitutable in the workplace with low-skilled native-born labor. Newly arrived immigrant labor is also substitutable with low-skilled immigrant workers who arrived in earlier waves."[14]

Bruce Nussbaum warns of the direction the economy is moving in his book, *The World After Oil*:

Immigration strikes at the very soul of this nation ...

and the problem can only get worse as we move into the twenty-first century. For it is cold, hard, inescapable truth that the last thing America is going to need in the years ahead is a flood of unskilled labor. As techno-casualties mount, a growing number of de-skilled people will be moving into the unskilled labor pool. At the same time, automation will eliminate a growing number of jobs. Hence a growing number of people, many of them furious at their new lower status in life, will be competing for a shrinking number of jobs.

In all but a very few instances, foreign professionals are not required for any present or likely future vacancies.

Keep in mind that one of the "Peace Dividends" deriving from the collapse of the Soviet Union is hundreds of thousands of lay-offs of highly trained professionals in defense-related industries, and the U.S. Armed Forces. The Army, Navy, and Air Force plan to eliminate more than 548,000 service and support positions over the next five years. An additional 2 million jobs are expected to be lost — over and above the most recent lay-offs — among civilians working in defense-related industries. There simply will not be a shortage of workers!

The Role of Employer Sanctions

Strict enforcement of employer sanctions (that provision of the 1986 Immigration Reform and Control Act that imposes penalties on employers who knowingly hire illegal aliens) would keep employers from hiring illegal aliens and force them to raise wages and improve working conditions, making these jobs more attractive to natives and recent legal immigrants. This would force sweatshops and those who violate child labor laws out of business.

Furthermore, it would spur technological innovation as industries strive to make workers more productive rather than relying on lowering wages to cut costs.

Summary

Given the changes the U.S. economy is undergoing, large-scale immigration is not in the national interest. A recent convert to this view is Michael Lind, executive editor of *The National Interest*. A past supporter of high levels of immigration, he has recently stated,

> *The economic argument against mass immigration now appears to me to be compelling. ...*
>
> *The U.S. economy, thanks to various long-term trends like automation and low-wage foreign competition, is not creating enough well-paid jobs for natives, much less for newcomers. Mass immigration only worsens this problem, by lowering wages which, in a tighter labor market, would naturally be higher, to the benefit of low-income Americans, or, if high wages encouraged the substitution of machinery for labor, to the benefit of the technological base within U.S. borders. (To prevent employers from relocating manufacturing and services to low-wage countries when entry-level American wages, following a steep reduction in immigration, begin to rise, deterrents to the expatriation of industry like a social tariff in some industries — preferably a common tariff shared by the U.S. and the European Community — might be necessary).*
>
> *...in today's economic circumstances the burden of proof should be shifted to those who argue for retaining a policy that permits great numbers of immigrants to compete with native and naturalized*

Americans for a diminishing number of good jobs. ...
*Tighter restrictions on immigration **are** the answer.*

We in the United States face an alternative. **Either** we incorporate our own recently displaced workers into an economy that places a premium on high-skill, high-wage enterprises (such as Japan's or Germany's), **or** we try to compete with Third World countries for low-pay, labor-intensive industries. Increasing immigration can only force us toward the latter alternative.

CHAPTER THREE
IMMIGRATION AND THE POLITICS
OF RACE, LANGUAGE, AND CULTURE

According to the INS, in 1992, 973,977 legal immigrants were admitted and placed on the road to citizenship. The record was set in 1991 when 1,827,167 were legally admitted. The figure for 1990 was 1,536,483. These bumper years follow a decade of record-setting immigration, and will likely be followed by numbers just as high as this decade unfolds, unless we change things. The previous high was set in 1907 at 1,285,349.[1]

Large scale immigration has been altering the distribution of power within the United States. It is shifting the balance between various ethnic and racial groups in our society, and it is redistributing power among the states and within each state.

It should be emphasized that the American public has never agreed to, nor was even consulted on, this massive shift. Nevertheless, it is proceeding full speed ahead, in a series of seemingly unrelated changes that reinforce one another and make each new step appear inevitable. Together, they add up to a massive alteration of our political, ethnic, and cultural landscape, one that is transforming the U.S. into a country that more and more Americans find alienating and bewildering.

The most fundamental change is the arrival, day by day, year by year, of very large numbers of immigrants who do not share our language or cultural values. As their numbers grow, so does their political influence and power, which they use in an attempt to derail any legislative movement to reduce immigration to a more manageable quantity.

Here is a catalogue of policies, both political and cultural, that derive from and reinforce high levels of immigration.

Counting Illegal Aliens for Reapportionment

Political power shifts created by immigration are said to be a *fait accompli*. They are translated into political power shifts through our decennial census. The census tallies the shifting population balance between and within the states, and the new statistical realities become the basis for apportioning seats in the federal and state legislatures.

As immigrants do not distribute themselves evenly across the country, the states (and communities within a state) that have acquired heavy concentrations of immigrants grow politically more powerful, thanks to their numbers. States not chosen by immigrants lose representation. California, Texas, and Florida — states that receive the preponderance of immigrants — have been gaining House of Representatives seats, at the expense of other states. These gains in political strength are accentuated by the practice of counting *illegal* aliens as well as legal aliens in the apportionment base.

The notion that people living in this country in violation of its laws should determine the allocation of political representation angers most citizens. The question of just who should be represented in Congress was extensively debated in the 1930s, when the issue was whether legally resident non-citizens should be counted for apportionment. It was finally decided to include all residents; however, this was before the age of massive illegal immigration, and the issue of legal versus illegal status was not debated.

The distortion brought about by including illegal aliens in the apportionment count operates at the state level as well as at the federal level. In fact, it may have its heaviest impact at the state representative (or assembly) district level; cities like Los Angeles and Miami, which are home to many illegal residents, are sending more legislators to Sacramento and Tallahassee than they would if illegal aliens were removed from the apportionment base.

Watering Down the English Language Requirements for Naturalization

The unwillingness to uphold even the most minimal standards of citizenship was signified clearly when Congress watered down the English requirement for citizenship. It started with the argument that some elderly Asian immigrants who, under laws passed early in this century, were ineligible for naturalization, now wanted to become citizens of the nation in which they had long resided. However, they had never learned English in their younger years, knowing that they could not aspire to citizenship.

Therefore, the argument went, an exception should be made allowing elderly long-time residents to naturalize without demonstrating a knowledge of English. Today, persons over fifty who have lived here for twenty or more years are excused from the very elementary English language test required for naturalization. A recent amendment offers this exemption to persons over fifty-five who have lived here fifteen years, as the requirements are progressively diluted.

In late 1993, the INS even conducted an entire naturalization ceremony in Spanish! This was one step too far for most people. It created a firestorm of protest that will likely end this practice, at least for the moment.[2]

Mandating Bilingual Ballots

In 1975, the Voting Rights Act was amended to require election officials to provide bilingual ballots and voting materials in any district, where 5 percent of the citizens of voting age were members of a single minority language group, and their illiteracy rate is higher than the national average. The definition of language minorities was limited to citizens of Spanish heritage, Asian Americans, American Indians and Alaskan Natives — speakers of European languages (other than Spanish) were pointedly excluded.

To be counted toward this requirement, residents of an area did *not* need to be U.S. citizens, and thus able to vote. Both resident aliens and illegal aliens were counted, to inflate the number of districts required to provide bilingual or even multilingual ballot materials.

Of course, the naturalization of citizens who had little knowledge of English had made bilingual ballots a logical next step. The law's supposed intent was to encourage more active participation by language minorities in the electoral process, but in practice, translating ballots has not improved voting rates among the favored groups.

In 1992, the bilingual ballot law was re-authorized and extended to the year 2007. A new triggering formula will make about a million more people eligible for bilingual electoral services, and add new languages to the ballot. Los Angeles, for example, now provides ballots in Chinese, Vietnamese, Tagalog (the language of the Philippines), Japanese, Spanish, in addition to English.[3]

Extending the Vote to Non-citizens

After effectively eliminating English as a requirement for naturalization and for voting by citizens, the next step presents itself quite naturally. Why not allow non-citizens the right to vote in elections? Preposterous though it may seem, this move is really a logical extension of all that has preceded it. It has already happened in Takoma Park, Maryland, a suburb of Washington, D.C., where residents narrowly approved a referendum giving aliens the right to vote in local elections.[4]

Now, this "Share the Vote" campaign to enfranchise aliens has been proposed for our nation's capital. As the proposed legislation has no mechanism for separating legal from illegal aliens, both would be able to vote. A forceful push for this new "right" is sure to continue.

Registering Voters Passively

America's low and declining voter turn-out has produced a number of schemes aimed at stimulating voter participation rates. Bilingual ballots, non-citizen voting, and mail-in postcard registration (available in some states) are all examples of this.

Political spokesmen for minority interests have now fastened upon registration as the main culprit for the low voter turn-out among minorities. The one-time act of registering a few days before an election, our traditional front-line defense against voting fraud, has been denounced as too burdensome and discriminatory.

At the insistence of ethnic politicians, a bill to make registration a passive and largely involuntary act passed the federal House and Senate in 1992. Registration would occur automatically, unless declined, whenever an individual applied for an automobile license or came in contact with any other state agency, such as the welfare department.

President Bush vetoed the bill, citing the potential for abuse and voter fraud. However, it was reintroduced in the next Congress and, with the help of six Republicans, passed the Senate. President Clinton signed HR2, the "Motor-Voter Bill," into law on May 20, 1993.[5]

Sixty-five special interest groups lobbied for its passage, including the Mexican-American Legal Defense and Education Fund (MALDEF), and the League of Women Voters. The Act explicitly discourages attempts to verify a voter registrant's citizenship by providing that mail-in registration forms "may not include any requirement for notarization or other formal authentication."

Guaranteeing Minority Legislative Seats

In 1982, the Voting Rights Act was amended to guarantee the election of minorities in areas of heavy minority settlement. This has meant the gerrymandering of electoral districts in such a way as to assure that minority candidates will win, despite poor minority voting records. The increase in minority representation in the national and state legislatures has been significant.

Hispanic politicians stand to gain most in this system. Their districts are home to large numbers of illegal aliens and legal resident aliens, who are not (yet) allowed to vote, but who are counted for setting up legislative districts. Further, since voter participation among Hispanic citizens has been low compared to those in more conventional districts, candidates in these districts win elections with very few votes.

For the Voting Rights Act to deliver guaranteed minority seats, it is necessary that minorities remain concentrated in ethnic ghettos that permit secure districts to be drawn. This clearly gives the political leadership an incentive to keep the population together, ghettoized, unassimilated and isolated from the mainstream of American society. Integration into the social, economic and intellectual life of American society constitutes a threat to ethnic leaders, for it will erode their power if their people melt into the American mainstream.

Admitting Puerto Rico to the Union of States

Puerto Rico, which has been a U.S. territory since 1898 and has enjoyed a great deal of autonomy since it became a "Commonwealth" in the 1950s, is now a serious candidate to become the 51st state of the Union.

A bill to grant statehood to Puerto Rico, a Spanish-speaking Caribbean island, without any prior agreement on language policy was defeated on a tie vote in a Senate committee in 1991. In 1992, opponents to statehood got the Puerto Rican legislature to remove English as one of the island's two official languages, leaving it officially monolingual in Spanish. They thought this would poison the chances for statehood.

However, popular sentiment in Puerto Rico for statehood is growing, fanned by talk of additional social programs that would come with statehood. In a plebiscite on the island on November 14, 1993, the statehood option barely lost out (46.3 percent of the vote) to the continuation of commonwealth status (48.5 percent). (The other votes were for independence.)

The admission to the union of a monolingual Spanish-speaking state would make for immense and long-term cultural and political problems. An immediate *political* consequence of statehood would be the addition of two U.S. Senators and somewhere between five and seven U.S. Representatives in the House, doubtless all Spanish speakers. Might they as a political maneuver (even if they speak English), demand simultaneous translations of debates in Congress, or call for publication of all government documents in Spanish as well as English? In Canada, it costs the government 19 cents Canadian for each word it translates between French and English, and as much as 30 cents Canadian for highly technical and mathematical documents[6] — think of the squadrons of translators required, the complaints about bad translations, the expense and delay!

Complications abound. How, for instance, would the Puerto Rican court systems operate? Doubtless in Spanish. But on appeal to the mainland, in addition to the usual expense of getting a transcript all parties can agree to, it would have to be translated into English. Faulty translation would become another basis for appeal ... as the old saying goes, "something was lost in the translation." Would Spanish-speaking attorneys be able to argue their cases before English-speaking judges? Perhaps we would see the revival of an early 1980s proposal for a separate Spanish language court system. (There was also a call for Spanish-speaking defendants to be tried only by a jury of their peers — that is, other Spanish speakers.)

A successful statehood bid by Puerto Rico could lead to the admission of other states to the Union. Like Puerto Rico, the U.S. territories of Guam, Samoa, and the Virgin Islands already have a "Resident Commissioner" sitting in the U.S. House of Representatives, who functions as a congressman. Though they do not vote on the floor, their votes in committee help determine the fate of legislation. If admitted, would these new states also want full "rights" for their historic languages?

Statehood for Puerto Rico is a step we should think through very carefully.

Next: Reinforcing Political Gains
Through Even More Immigration

Large-scale immigration has generated major power shifts in the United States — and still more immigration will confirm, expand and consolidate these shifts.

The amnesty program enacted in 1989 legalized 3.1 million illegal immigrants, and put them on the road to eventual citizenship, to be granted in this decade.

A second amnesty was declared in 1990 when Congress allowed the spouses and children of the previously amnestied aliens to stay in the United States, even though these relatives had not met the criteria set for the initial amnesty. This added many more millions to our population. By the mid-1990s, many of these people will have become citizens and will be able to petition in turn for the admission of *their* relatives, further extending the immigration chain.

Also, as we explain in Chapter Seven, the 1990 bill became the focus of intense pro-immigration lobbying. It ended up becoming a vehicle for expanding legal immigrant admissions by 40 percent, to nearly one million per year.

In the absence of moves to strengthen employer sanction laws and with the North American Free Trade Agreement (NAFTA) signed into law in 1993 without consideration of the implications for immigration, the projections are for continued high levels of legal and illegal immigration. Unless we act, another record-breaking decade is ahead, one that may well see some 15 million new immigrants settling in our midst.

Institutionalizing Ethnic Divisions

Political power shifts are sustained by cultural ones, which in turn have political consequences. The most notable cultural policies are those that affect language. Some of these have already been discussed, but several others are of major importance:

Bilingual Education

In 1968, Congress passed the Bilingual Education Act, providing federal funding to school systems struggling to educate non-English-speaking children. It authorized instruction in the students' native tongue as a bridge to English.

In 1974, the Supreme Court decided in *Lau v. Nichols* that students who do not know English must be given special assistance in school. The nature of this assistance was not specified. Several possible methods were mentioned as acceptable, including bilingual education.

Within the federal agencies, however, the *Lau* decision was interpreted as a mandate for bilingual education. It was initially sold as a transitional program that would quickly lead immigrant children to the regular English curriculum. However, a bilingual education establishment quickly grew up and wanted to retain students in their native language environment for much of their schooling. In addition, maintaining the students' culture now has become a goal of bilingual education.

This is *not* just a question of Spanish. In California, the public schools are struggling to educate students in more than 80 languages. In the Washington, D.C. area, it is not uncommon for teachers to have a dozen language groups represented in a classroom.[7]

The educational results of this segregation by language have been disappointing, especially in learning English. Politically, however, the existence of a body of young people uncomfortable in English and alienated from the mainstream serves the purposes of ethnic politicians very well.

Multicultural Education

Multicultural education has become the code word for teaching history and social studies in a manner sure to develop in minority children a sense of estrangement from mainstream American society.

Students are taught that their ancestors have been the victims of persecution and injustice in this country, that they themselves are not valued and that their own culture is better than the public culture to which generations of immigrants have assimilated. This approach is rationalized as building self-esteem, which is supposedly the key to scholastic success. The children's "alienation" from other Americans helps sharpen their ethnic awareness and reinforces power relationships based on minority status.

Puerto Rican Statehood

As already mentioned, the admission of Puerto Rico as a Spanish-speaking state would immediately help consolidate Hispanic political power. It would also have enormous political and cultural implications, most obviously that the United States would instantly become an officially bilingual country, much like Canada. Doubtless, other language groups would then make their claims, putting us on the road to a disastrous multilingualism.

This development would also be a major turning point in the reapportionment of economic as well as political power. In Canada, which became officially bilingual in 1969, the economic value of a minority language has grown substantially.

The Canadian government must now function in two languages, and — reasonably enough under such circumstances — the top government posts have been designated as officially bilingual. As French-speakers were much more likely to be bilingual than English-speakers, French Canadians have now occupied these high government positions in disproportionate numbers.[8] In fact, Francophones, who constitute 24 percent of the country's population, have captured up to two-thirds and even three-quarters of the upper-level official bilingual jobs in many federal departments. Once entrenched, they perpetuate the bilingual system.

We could expect a similar wholesale transfer of government jobs in the United States should we ever become officially bilingual, as the unconditional acceptance of Puerto Rico as a state would make us.

The North American Free Trade Agreement

The NAFTA will have important consequences which are the subject of heated disputes between various economic, environmental, labor, and other interests. It will also affect the flow of immigrants to the U.S.

Philip Martin, University of California-Davis immigration scholar, foresees a jump in migration as Mexico adjusts to NAFTA, particularly as Mexican corn farmers are undercut by cheaper American corn. Eventually, in a decade or so, he thinks it possible that immigration pressure could subside, as Mexico undergoes economic development. Whether this is just wishful thinking remains to be seen.[9]

But ultimately NAFTA's weightiest impact may be cultural — not in the sense of increased cultural exchanges, which we should welcome, but rather in the sense of permanently altered perceptions. Will it, in effect, dissolve the border between these two very different countries, and gradually erode our own identity as citizens of a well-defined unique nation? Will it lead to a vague general awareness that we are just part of a North American no-man's land, with various groups contending for pieces of the pie?

Summary

All these seemingly unrelated developments are ripening, reinforcing one another, and leading to an uncertain future. Our country is undergoing rapid and unplanned change, and is fast becoming unrecognizable to those many Americans who, in 1965, were not consulted nor sufficiently warned about what might lay ahead.

CHAPTER FOUR
IMMIGRATION AND CRIME

The hard evidence is that criminal aliens are committing serious crimes, leaving and re-entering the justice system.
— Michael D. Antonovich
Board of Supervisors, Los Angeles County
May 14, 1992

Crime and immigrants. The combination of those two words may be jarring to many readers. To link the two is to challenge deep mythologies about immigrants as heroic, hard-working people who come to U.S. shores to improve life for themselves, and in the process improve it for all Americans. While the myth continues to contain elements of truth, it fails to provide a fully accurate portrait of the millions of foreign citizens who move to our country. Public policy decisions about the future of this country must be made on practical, not mythological, assessments. Immigration indeed also has a selfish and even seamy aspect. And no subject more quickly gets to the heart of that aspect than crime.

Other chapters of this book show how immigrants who match our best mythological descriptions inadvertently still bring harm to the United States merely by their numbers. The book also shows how a portion of immigrants eventually decide that their only way to pursue the American dream is by having the American people pay for it through the system of public social service.

But a frightening portion of immigrants have decided that instead of working for the dream they will try to steal it.

To make such a statement of fact is to risk charges of immigrant-bashing and mean-spiritedness. In this chapter we do not imply that all or most immigrants are law-breakers. But the factual record is revealing: many immigrants do commit crimes. And under current immigration laws, a disconcerting number of newcomers actually arrive with the plan that crime will be their avenue to the American dream. And all illegal aliens show at least some propensity for crime by their very presence, possible only through the violation of at least one law.

The information that follows here likely will anger and perhaps shock the reader. If it does, the prime target of wrath should not be the immigrants but the public officials who persist in perpetuating an immigration system that allows such outrageous results.

Criminal Alien Activities Escalating

Criminal activities committed by aliens have escalated dramatically. Aliens are crowding local, state, and federal jails across the country. The U.S. Bureau of Prisons reports that more than 25 percent of federal inmates are non-U.S. citizens, from over 120 countries. Half were convicted on drug offenses and most are subject to deportation.

"If we think the [number of imprisoned illegals] is high, what is worse is that seven out of eight [criminal] aliens are either released or given probation and never serve time in prison," explained Representative Lamar Smith (R-Texas), a member of the House Judiciary Subcommittee on Immigration, Refugees and International Law.

For the U.S. population as a whole, the incarceration rate in federal and state prisons is 233 per 100,000 persons. Among illegal aliens, the incarceration rate is three times the U.S. average. Since 1980, there has been a 600 percent increase in alien inmates, principally for drug-related offenses. Over the past five years, an average of more than 72,000 aliens have been arrested annually on drug charges.[1]

These statistics do not imply that all or most immigrants are law-breakers. But under current immigration laws and procedures, frighteningly large numbers of newcomers see crime as their avenue to the American dream.

Foreign Crime Syndicates Target U.S.

The FBI warns that international crime and terrorist organizations have placed America under siege. Gary Renick, Assistant District Director for INS Investigations, San Antonio, Texas, noted that crime bosses in such places as Colombia, Mexico, Nigeria, South Korea, Japan, and Hong Kong view the U.S. as an especially inviting "land of opportunity." According to the INS, organized criminals of each nationality seem to specialize: Colombians in cocaine; Mexicans in marijuana, alien smuggling, and auto theft; Nigerians in heroin, student-loan and credit-card fraud; Chinese in heroin and alien smuggling; South Koreans in prostitution; Russians in drugs and insurance-fraud; Jamaicans in cocaine.[2]

Since the mid-1980s, major crime operations have not only come to be directed by foreign nationals, but staffed by them as well, instead of employing American agents. An INS report titled, *The Newest Criminals: The Emergence of Non-Traditional Organized Ethnic Crime Groups and INS's Role in Combating Them*, says that many of the ethnic criminal organizations exist in their native countries and simply expand into the United States. Said David Leroy, chief of domestic intelligence for the U.S. Drug Enforcement Administration, "Ethnic gangs appear to be *the* new trend in crime."

Criminal activities in the U.S. run by Third World natives can be traced back to the Immigration Act of 1965 and failure to control illegal immigration. The social effects of the 1965

Act were not felt immediately. Only after a "critical mass" of foreign colonists arrived here did law enforcement agencies begin to learn about the presence of criminal elements among the new immigrants. As *U.S. News & World Report* conceded, "it is startling the degree to which the clout of newer ethnic gangs is reflective of immigration trends."[3]

Asian Criminal Organizations

The Triads

The Triads date back to the 17th century, when patriotic Han Chinese founded secret societies to fight the foreign Manchu invaders and restore the Ming dynasty. By the end of the 19th century, many Triads had largely abandoned their political idealism and transformed themselves into sophisticated criminal enterprises. Leading politicians, including Dr. Sun Yat-sen and Chiang Kai-shek, found it expedient to trade favors with the powerful Triads, whose opportunities for profits improved after the Manchus were finally overthrown in 1911.

Triads have been active in Hong Kong since 1842. During World War II, they often cooperated with the Japanese. In time, they came to control the dockyards, and were able to penetrate other labor markets. After Mao-Tse-Tung seized power on the mainland in 1949, other Triads moved to Macao (the Portuguese colony near Hong Kong that comes under the authority of Beijing in 1999), and Taiwan. Today, most Triads are based in Hong Kong and Taiwan, with branches operating in other parts of Asia, Europe, Canada, and the United States. According to the Royal Hong Kong Police Force, approximately fifty Triad societies are based in Hong Kong, with a combined membership of some 300,000. One society, the 14 K Triad, has nearly 40,000 members. The State of California Attorney General's Office reports that the Wo Hop To Triad, which is one of the most active Triads in California, has a combined membership of 28,000.[4]

Alien smuggling has become an important part of Triad work. *The Washington Post* reported on February 9, 1993, that more than sixty international routes are used to illegally bring 100,000 Chinese nationals into the U.S. each year (and additional tens of thousands into Canada and Australia as well). The individuals pay huge fees to the professional smugglers, often ranging from $25,000 to $50,000. Those who are unable to pay in advance settle their debt by becoming indentured to Triad-controlled businesses in America, especially garment sweatshops, prostitution rings, gambling operations, and drug dealing.

Writing in *The Christian Science Monitor*, December 24, 1991, Ann Scott Tyson revealed that, "The Chinese groups tend to specialize in certain kinds of crime in big cities. Fujianese criminals in New York tend to be involved in violent crime. Cantonese from China's Guangdong Province operate vice and extortion rackets in San Francisco, and Taiwanese crime groups are active in money laundering and white collar crime in Los Angeles and Houston."

The Triads' most important source of wealth derives from their control of the major supplies of heroin. The hilly area bordering Burma, Laos, and Thailand, known as the "Golden Triangle," is where over 70 percent of the world's opium is grown. As investigator Gerald Posner points out in his study of the Triads, *Warlords of Crime*, "Without heroin they are just another group of criminals. With heroin they have a potential for profit unmatched in the annals of organized crime."

The FBI reports that Asian youth gangs, notably Vietnamese "refugees" and their American-born offspring, employed as "street muscle" by the Triads, operate in the U.S. through Tongs.[5] (The word "Tong," derived from "Town Hall," describes fronts that often publicly engage in charitable work in Chinese communities.) These Asian syndicates pose special problems for law enforcement, since their members are bound to secrecy, and because the almost insurmountable barriers of language, dialect, and culture make law enforcement difficult in the extreme — including reading arrestees their Miranda rights, not just in the proper language, but in the correct dialect!

Federal officials say that New York City has become the central hub for Chinese criminal activity — operations that extend to Boston, Philadelphia, Dallas, Houston, and Portland. San Francisco and Los Angeles are their West Coast headquarters.

The forthcoming transfer of control of Hong Kong to Communist China in 1997 has spurred a flight from the colony. Organized crime has flourished in Hong Kong since the end of World War II. But Asian crime lords fear that Beijing may exercise tighter control than the British have. Among those seeking refuge elsewhere are the Triads, whose destinations of preference are the United States, Canada, and Australia. Some Triad chiefs, known as "dragon heads," are suspected of trying to take advantage of the new visa category that permits immigration by individuals who promise to invest $1 million in the U.S. (the actual source of investment funds is often masked).

The Wah Ching

The Wah Ching is a one-time street gang that has evolved into a sophisticated organized crime group. With international ties to Hong Kong and Taiwan Triads, its U.S. base of operations is San Francisco, with powerful factions working out of other California cities, including Monterey Park, Los Angeles, and Oakland.

Like the Triads, the Wah Ching is engaged in gambling, prostitution, extortion, infiltration of businesses, and drug trafficking. They also own myriad legitimate businesses.

Membership in the Wah Ching is growing, thanks in large part to their active recruitment of Viet Ching gang members.

"Viet Ching" are gangs made up of youths who are ethnic Chinese from Vietnam.

In his annual report to the legislature, *Organized Crime in California*, the state Attorney General details Wah Ching activities, including their growing involvement in *pai gow* gambling (pai gow is a Chinese high-stakes game played with domino tiles). Through the California-based Productions Entertainment Company, they also play a major role in the Chinese entertainment industry, which includes arranging concert tours in the U.S. of Oriental acts, as well as distributing Chinese video cassettes in this country. Overseas tours are controlled by the San Yee On Triad of Hong Kong. Triads control the worldwide distribution of Chinese videos originating in Hong Kong and Taiwan.[6]

The Yakuza

The Yakuza are the Japanese crime syndicates. According to Japan's National Police Agency they have well over 100,000 members divided among 3,300 "families" and federations. Four years ago, their annual income was estimated to exceed $10 billion. Among Asian criminals today, they rank second only to the Chinese Triads in power.[7]

In the United States, as elsewhere, they are involved in drug smuggling, gunrunning (to Japan), extortion, money laundering, pornography, and prostitution. The California Attorney General warns that they are reinvesting the proceeds from their criminal activities in legitimate businesses throughout this country. The Securities and Exchange Commission, in July, 1991, revealed that President George Bush's brother, Prescott, acted as a consultant for companies controlled by Yakuza godfather Susumu Ishii that were interested in buying small American firms.[8]

Over twenty years ago, Yakuza started "casing" the state of Hawaii. As David Kaplan and Alec Dubro observe in their book, *Yakuza: Japan's Criminal Underworld*, "Given the dollar value of Yakuza-related enterprises, Hawaii is becoming dependent on Yakuza investment. ... The money is now part of the economic structure of the islands. ... It is in Hawaii, perhaps, that the future can best be seen, where a panoply of Eastern and Western gangsters cooperate."

Caribbean Criminals

Jamaican Posses

According to *U.S. News & World Report*, Jamaican criminals are "probably the most active after the Asians among the newer ethnic gangs." Known as *posses*, they got their start smuggling marijuana into the U.S. They moved into cocaine after discovering the huge profits to be made dealing that product. In many American cities Jamaicans now dominate the crack market. As Al Lamberti of the Broward (Florida) Sheriff's Department pointed out, "They're moving American blacks off the street corners. And they're ready to use whatever violence is necessary to do the job." James Scott of the Miami-Dade police added, "We've worked with all sorts of ethnic groups involved in the drug trade — Cubans, Colombians, American blacks. But none of these have the weaponry the Jamaicans do."[9]

Over thirty *posses* have been identified by law enforcement agencies. Some of the bigger gangs, such as the "Spangler" and "Shower" *posses*, are now involved in the international gunrunning trade.

Many of these Jamaican gangsters are adherents of the Rastafarian religious cult and have been enormously successful, particularly in Brooklyn. Newcomer criminals from Panama have mimicked Rastafarian hair locks and dress as a way of breaking into their drug operations.

Haitians

North America is now home to a Haitian population equalling nearly one-sixth of Haiti's 6.3 million people. A loosely structured network of Haitian criminals is engaged in drug dealing, car thefts, and armed robberies. A major source of income is prostitution.

In late 1990, as reported in the *Montreal Gazette*, the Montreal, Quebec police broke a notorious cross-border gang that operated in Canada and the United States. Hundreds of Haitians were arrested who had forced into prostitution young Canadian and U.S. women, a number of whom were taken from foster homes. They were subjected to unspeakable treatment.

It is noteworthy that many of the Haitians who have engaged in crime originally came to the U.S. as refugees, or were recruited by the Quebec Immigration Ministry when it sought to bring in more French-speaking people. On both sides of the border, many Haitian neighborhoods have become violent, crime-ridden slums. French language newspapers have coined a new word to describe the transformation: *se bronxifier* — to become like the Bronx.

U.S. law enforcement officials report that members of the dread *ton-ton macoutes* (Haiti's secret police) are engaged in criminal activity in Florida, and elsewhere.

Cubans

In the spring of 1980, Fidel Castro opened the Cuban port of Mariel to those wishing to leave. Among the 125,000 who took advantage of this opportunity to migrate to the United States were thousands of criminals, sex offenders, and mental patients. Police officials and fellow refugees place the number of undesirables at 40,000. Few Marielitos brought records with them. Often, U.S. authorities could not even verify their names.

The Cubans who arrived here in the 1980 boatlift differ dramatically from the first waves of refugees who came over between 1959-1962. The Marielitos were younger, less-educated, poorer, included fewer families, and had fewer U.S. ties.

From Miami, Marielito crime has spread across America. According to a report prepared by the Las Vegas Police Department, "a national conspiracy exists" among Cuban "refugee" criminals. They have specialized in such crimes as airline ticket fraud, credit card fraud, and drug dealing.

Local police officials from around the country complain that the federal government has done little to aid them in combatting refugee-related crime. For reasons that remain unclear, the Federal Bureau of Investigation does not collect information on refugee crime. As a spokesman for the FBI, Manuel Marquez, said, "It's just not our problem."

Few of the Marielitos who have committed felonies in the United States have been expelled, as federal law mandates. Over the past twelve years, the government has engaged in largely fruitless negotiations with the Cuban dictator, but only a few felons actually have been returned. Castro has made it clear that he does not want them back. And, ethnic lobbyists and civil rights activists have created further impediments to deporting anybody to Cuba. In the meantime, Cuban criminals detained at U.S. prisons staged destructive uprisings in 1987 and 1991.

The results of a poll conducted by Mason-Dixon Opinion Research should come as no surprise: 77 percent of the non-Hispanic whites and 72 percent of the non-Hispanic blacks said the quality of life in Florida has been hurt by emigration from Cuba. Only 1 percent said they believe Florida has been helped by Cuban emigration.

Other Newer Ethnic Gangs

Russian Emigres

"Organized crime," says Stephen Handelman of Columbia University, "is the most explosive force to emerge from the wreckage of Soviet Communism."[10] *Insight* magazine reports that, "among the 200,000 Soviet immigrants in the United States, most of whom are Jewish emigres, the so-called 'Russian mafia' has shown a penchant for get-rich schemes and a ready willingness to use extreme violence to back up their operations."[11]

According to the President's Commission on Organized Crime, Soviet authorities took advantage of special emigration rights granted to Jews and, over the past twenty years, "included a significant number of criminals who were forced to leave Russia." The Presidential Commission suggested that by means of Jewish emigration, "The Soviet Union attempted to empty their prisons and rid their society of undesirables, much as Fidel Castro did several years later during the Mariel boatlift."

Federal authorities estimate that at least a dozen Russian gangs operate out of the greater New York area, with the Brighton Beach section of Brooklyn serving as their headquarters. Other groups are based in Los Angeles, San Francisco, Portland, Dallas, Miami, Chicago, Cleveland, Boston, and Philadelphia.[12]

Their activities include extortion, loan-sharking, counterfeiting, arson, insurance fraud, burglary, murder-for-hire, and cocaine and heroin dealing. Cooperating with the Italian Mafia, they have become increasingly involved in the bootleg gasoline trade. Distributors deliver gasoline to service stations, but fail to pass on the federal excise taxes collected. In November, 1991, a leading Russian emigre gangster, Oleg Yasko, was convicted in California for skimming 40 cents in unpaid taxes on each gallon of gasoline his company delivered to other wholesalers and retail service stations. In February, 1994, a gang led by Yakov Litvak was arrested in Fort Lauderdale, Florida. He and his cohorts conspired to sell 130,500 gallons of gasoline and 6.3 million gallons of diesel fuel without paying taxes. Said an FBI agent, "Some of the schemes are so complicated, even we don't understand them."[13]

In July, 1991, federal authorities broke one of the biggest cases of medical fraud in history, when they arrested the twelve leaders of Michael and David Smushkevichs' emigre ring. Michael traveled around the world with passports from the Soviet Union, Israel, and Mexico. The Smushkevichs used mobile medical clinics to attract patients with promises of free tests, and then billed some 1,400 insurance companies for over $1 billion in phony claims. "It ranks right up with the Drexel Burnham insider stock trading case," said David Smith, head of the Postal Inspection Service in Los Angeles.

The *Los Angeles Times* reports that "ill-gotten gains in this country are being shipped back home (to Russia) to some of the estimated 5,000 crime syndicates there so they can get an upper hand economically as the once-communist economies move to a free market." Displaced former members of the KGB are suspected of being involved.

The U.S. Justice Department considers the Russian gangs to be an "emerging crime problem." On April 14, 1992, the newly formed federal task force on Russian emigre crime held its first meeting in Los Angeles.

Like other ethnic criminal organizations, Russian gangs have evolved through three major stages: extortion of their own people; expansion into other crimes; and movement into legitimate businesses.

Israelis

Organized crime in Israel reached a peak in the mid-1970s. Vigorous police work encouraged the Israeli crime element to emigrate. Many moved to the United States. In the

Northeast, Florida, and on the West Coast, Israeli gangs, "comprised mostly of Sephardic Jews born in Arab countries, are increasingly active in the U.S. heroin trade," according to *U.S. News & World Report*.

Los Angeles County sheriff Sherman Block told *The Jerusalem Post* that the potent Israeli mafia has spread across America, graduating from extorting money from poor and elderly Jews — many of them former concentration camp inmates — to major drug dealing and fraud schemes against the wealthy. A veteran Drug Enforcement Administration agent testified, "We have seen Israelis buying heroin in Pakistan, Turkey and Thailand. We are now seeing their ability to interact with other criminal groups, including La Cosa Nostra [and] the Chinese." Peter Moses and Carl Pelleck reported in *The New York Post* that while the Israelis currently deal mainly in heroin, they are now moving into cocaine.[14]

Nigerians

Nigerian citizens, many of whom enter on student visas, are part of an international crime syndicate headquartered in Washington, D.C. and now active across the country. They specialize in huge drug deals and major fraud schemes, and are among the most violent of criminals.

The Nigerians have obtained a growing share of the American heroin trade. Much of the contraband enters the U.S. through Customs via Canada into New York and Michigan. In 1990, one of the biggest heroin busts recorded in the Midwest involved Ojo Adighibe, a Nigerian living in Grand Rapids, Michigan, who had heroin stashed in typewriters shipped to his stateside address from his homeland.[15]

Law enforcement authorities admit that Nigerians are difficult to deal with. They tend to organize locally into small "cells" of five to twelve members, each headed by a boss. Members often are relatives or members of the same tribe —

frequently Ibo or Yoruba. They like to cooperate with each other. If apprehended, few will inform on their fellow cell members.

Furthermore, federal authorities do not keep track of foreign "students" to see that they remain registered in school and are attending classes. Nigerian students recruited by criminal gangs will often remain in school, but reduce their course load. Others stop attending altogether. Student visas are issued for up to five years and the U.S. government has no mechanism in place to monitor the holder's compliance with the law.

Nigerians are among the foremost perpetrators of credit card fraud. A California police report on the "Nigerian mafia" discloses that they are responsible for over $1 billion in credit card losses every year. An "African church" in Los Angeles fronts as a training school, where Nigerian immigrants are taught the niceties of this trade. One method used to obtain credit card information illegally is to take employment in hospitals, hotels, post offices, and the mail rooms of corporations and apartments. There they can acquire names, addresses, and social security numbers, which are then used to apply for credit cards or to divert existing accounts by contacting credit card issuers and giving them a new address. Phony letters of credit are also employed to gain access to our financial network.

One ring was broken by Houston, Texas, postal authorities in August, 1991. Nigerian Ikembe Azikiwe offered letter carriers $3,000 for each MasterCard or Visa Goldcard they turned over, and 50 percent of the value of any large commercial checks they were able to steal. Azikiwe boasted that a friend of his, engaged in the same work in Chicago, was able to steal enough in one week to pay cash for a new Mercedes. The U.S. Postal Inspection Service, in its *Law Enforcement Report* (Fall 1991) pointed out that, "attempted bribery of postal employees is being conducted on a relatively large scale basis by criminal elements within the Nigerian community."

Even when they are arrested, many Nigerians, like other felons, are released on bond and then fail to show up for trial. Lawyers representing bonding companies sometimes make up false death certificates, reporting that their client has died and asking for bond release.[16]

Costs High For Three Big States

The impact of the new alien crime wave is being felt nationwide, but is acute in states with large alien populations. And the dollar costs do not adequately reflect the burden on society of additional crime. The administration of justice — including bilingual interpreters and court-appointed attorneys — is bogged down by the necessity of dealing with foreign-born criminals.

California
- State and local governments in California spend more than $500 million a year to arrest, try, and imprison illegal aliens who commit serious crimes, according to a California state Senate report issued on March 23, 1993.

- The annual legal costs of dealing with all types of crimes by illegal aliens could run as high as $1.5 billion, according to an estimate included in the report.

- The California Attorney General reports that approximately 16,000 illegal alien felons are incarcerated in state prisons. Every year it costs California taxpayers $350 million to keep these criminal aliens behind bars.

- A 1992 study commissioned by the San Diego Association of Governments found that one in four jail inmates acknowledged being in this country illegally.

Judges estimate that up to 35 percent of the felony cases in Superior Court involve illegals. A 1990 check in felony disposition court discovered that 41 percent of the defendants had immigration "holds" — on completion of sentence, they would be released to the INS for detention.

- As a test, Orange County Superior Court Judge David O. Carter invited the INS into his courtroom to help identify criminal aliens and develop deportation cases against them. Judge Carter informed the U.S. House Judiciary Committee that "the results are staggering. ... My criminal calendar is 36 percent illegal felons. These statistics would be much higher except the INS does not place holds on illegal felons who have started the amnesty process or come from countries where the United States is an adversary and has no extradition authority. Vietnam, Cambodia, Iran, and Cuba are some of the most obvious countries which will not accept extradited felons."

- Orange County Police Chief Merrill Duncan disclosed during a press conference in April, 1992, that the 12 percent increase in crime from the previous year in that city is the result of a "tremendous influx of illegal aliens." He added that, "most crime suspects are illegals."[17]

New York

- Twelve percent of the over 64,000 inmates in New York's state correctional system are foreign-born (either illegal aliens or legally admitted aliens who have committed crimes). The Governor's office reports it costs taxpayers $210 million a year to house these criminals. Foreign-born felons come from 111 different countries around the world. Nearly half of the foreign-born inmates in New York come from Caribbean nations, with 29 percent hailing from the Dominican Republic.

- On April 27, 1992, the state of New York filed a suit against the federal government, demanding that it start taking custody of thousands of illegal aliens currently incarcerated in state prisons. The suit charges that the federal government is responsible for taking charge of these inmates and launching deportation proceedings against them. But too often, the U.S. Justice Department fails to do so. Once convicts serve their terms, the state is forced to simply release them onto the streets, where they are often arrested for new crimes.

- Between April 1, 1985 and December 31, 1992, the number of foreign-born inmates in New York rose 194 percent.

- Foreign-born inmates are more likely to have been convicted of drug offenses and more serious crimes of violence than inmates born in the United States.[18]

Texas

In the Texas state prison system, only 4.3 percent of the inmates are known to be foreign-born. But this is because, as *The Dallas Morning News* pointed out on February 2, 1992, "the state in effect uses municipal and county jails to house some of its prisoners. In the largest jail on the Texas-Mexico border, the county facility at El Paso, criminal aliens range from 10 to 15 percent of the inmate population. Of the federal inmates in Texas, 36 percent are foreign-born." How extensively aliens are involved in crime throughout the state is difficult to determine, since many jurisdictions, such as Dallas, keep no statistics on the nationality of criminals.

Street Gangs

As "refugee" communities have sprung up across the nation, new ethnically based youth gangs have emerged. They are heavily involved in the drug trade and are responsible for a growing portion of the violence that wracks America's metropolitan areas.

This gang culture belies the media-created image of immigrants as "model citizens." For example, in California, as reported by *The New York Times*, "the simmering ethnic stew pot that is Los Angeles seems to favor youth gang activity. Gangs of almost every nationality flourish: Samoan, Filipino, Salvadoran, Mexican, Korean, Vietnamese. Experts estimate there are about 600 gangs." Law enforcement officials put the current number of members for these gangs at over 100,000. In nearby Long Beach, a war between Cambodian and Hispanic gangs has been raging for over two years.

Street gang membership by non-Hispanic whites is rare. For example, in Los Angeles, fully 57 percent of criminal gang members are Hispanic and 36 percent are black. In Denver, where whites make up 80 percent of the population, 60 percent of the gang members are black (although they are only 5 percent of the city's population) and 33 percent are Hispanics (who represent 12 percent of Denver's population).[19]

Gang activity is no longer limited to the traditional areas of immigrant settlement. As new immigrants have migrated to the Midwest, America's heartland has come to experience the ethnic violence that plagues the East and West Coasts, Florida, and the Southwest. In Chicago, the police are doing battle against not only black and Hispanic gangs, but Assyrians, Chinese, Cambodians, Vietnamese, Filipinos, and Greeks.

Symptomatic of the trend, St. Paul, Minnesota, law enforcement officials have called for tough measures to combat Asian teen crime in the wake of a rash of major burglaries, including theft from gun shops. Special programs to divert

Asian youth from lives of crime have been authorized by the state legislature in an effort to manage the problem.

The western Michigan communities of Holland and Grand Rapids are experiencing a rise in violence attributable to young Asian males. A confidential police memo circulated in 1991 identified several gangs operating locally and regionally, such as "38 Crew," "Oriental Posse," "Crips With an Attitude," and "BBC" (Born Before Christ). Police admit that they have been reluctant to discuss the problem openly. The area has seen a huge increase in its Asian population, "many of them church-sponsored immigrants," *The Grand Rapids Press* reported.[20]

As bad as the situation is now, the problems created in the U.S. by our new immigrant street gangs are bound to become much worse in the future if corrective measures--including immigration reform--are not quickly enacted and strictly enforced.

Cross-border Auto Theft

Along our border with Mexico, auto theft has become a multi-billion dollar growth industry. Thieves in California and Texas communities, including some Mexican law enforcement officers, charge several hundred dollars to steal cars and zip across the border to Mexico. Teens are favored as drivers, since they face little more than a mild rebuke if arrested.

High-priced luxury cars and off-road vehicles, such as Jeeps and Broncos, are prized. The cars are shipped from Mexico to buyers in Latin America, Europe, and the Middle East. Before the Persian Gulf war, many vehicles were bound for Kuwait.

Because U.S. Customs does not check identification of outgoing cars, it is relatively easy for thieves to cross the Mexican border headed south. "It's almost a license to steal," Lt. Bob Samples of the Los Angeles Police Department remarked.

The War on Drugs

The celebrated U.S. "war on drugs" has been three-pronged: trying to eradicate drugs where they are grown and manufactured, called "going to the source;" a nationwide education effort to discourage drug use by youngsters; stepped up law enforcement. Thus far, the campaign has not had much success. Despite generous increases in foreign aid to countries where cocaine, heroin, and marijuana are produced, production has soared. This is hardly surprising, given that profits generated by the drug trade are far greater than those deriving from other cash crops.

When faced with issues that require decisive action, Americans have come to rely on "education" as the preferred, safe response. While the "Just Say No!" campaign may have heightened public awareness, such education has proved to be a remarkable failure among those elements of the U.S. population most inclined to use drugs. Drug use is actually growing.

Law enforcement agencies nationwide have been overwhelmed by drug-related crime. Courts are backlogged for years. Even with special "drug courts," other pressing cases are delayed for months and even years. Many serious crimes are being plea bargained away by local prosecutors, and others are not even taken to court just to clear the docket. Our jails and prisons are overflowing with inmates convicted of drug-related offenses.

No matter how much apologists for our open immigration policy may wish to obfuscate the issue, we cannot separate our illegal drug and immigration problems from one another. Back in 1986, then Attorney General Edwin Meese informed Congress that, "The reality is that immigration is contributing to the drug problem." He pointed out that drug smugglers "get lost in the crowd" of aliens crossing the border and that traffickers regularly use aliens to transport drugs into the U.S.

The international dimension of the drug trade in America highlights the failure of past policies to protect the nation's interests. Federal officials concede that foreign nationals not only are responsible for producing virtually all of the drugs consumed in the U.S., but are in charge of nearly all of the distribution.

Cocaine, and its inexpensive, smokeable derivative, *crack*, is produced in the Andes, refined in Colombia and Mexico, and distributed worldwide by Colombian drug lords who cooperate with other foreign nationals, including Panamanians, Nicaraguans, Mexicans, Jamaicans, Dominicans, Haitians, Nigerians, Indians, Pakistanis, and Asians.

Florida remains a major hub for their North American operations. The drug trade has pumped billions of dollars into the Sunshine State's economy. But as Florida, which sits astride the major air and trade routes from South America, has come under increasing surveillance by law enforcement, our porous border with Mexico has become the path favored by foreign suppliers. As one Colombian drug dealer told a Miami-based colleague, "Come to California. It's the promised land."

All along the border, from California through Texas, small communities have sprung up that serve as staging areas for the U.S.-bound shipments. Mexican *burros* smuggle drugs across the border. As Tom McDermott of the U.S. Customs Service explained, "There are a lot of advantages" to using Mexican routes. "They can stage loads in Mexico with little or no risk, and they have a nice interstate highway system to get to their markets."

The drug trade generates billions of dollars in profits, with an increasing portion being reinvested in the U.S. and used to purchase real estate and legitimate businesses.

Although it is viewed as a "friendly" country by many Americans, Mexico remains among the top sources of heroin and marijuana, and the major supply route for cocaine. Mexico

City routinely promises to cooperate with U.S.-sponsored anti-drug efforts. William van Raab, customs chief under President Reagan, is among those who charge that official complicity in the international drug trade reaches high levels of the Mexican government.[21] The White House and State Department have been reluctant to highlight the role played by ranking Mexican political figures in the drug commerce.

In the wake of the North American Free Trade Agreement (NAFTA), labor columnist Gus Tyler reports that, "The narco-traficantes are buying up *maquiladoras* — Mexican-based plants that assemble component parts from America and then ship the finished product to America. The smugglers load the finished product on to trucks that they own and that will now have the right to roll unobstructed into this country. No need to suggest what will be concealed on those trucks."[22]

Cocaine and marijuana are only two of the most popular drugs being smuggled into the U.S. Heroin continues to generate billions of dollars of profits annually. Since President Nixon declared his own "war on drugs" in 1971, the number of heroin addicts in this country has increased by several hundred thousand. In a number of metropolitan areas, nearly three-quarters of urban crime is committed by heroin users. The millions of dollars spent on anti-heroin education have done little to discourage heroin use. Only the deadly disease AIDS has actually reduced the number of junkies. Dealers have now developed a smokeable version of heroin, which they have already introduced to America.

As with cocaine, the burgeoning heroin trade is dominated by aliens. *The New York Times* reported, "As the Mafia's role declines, the multi-billion-dollar heroin trade is increasingly being conducted by criminal organizations that together sound like a United Nations of drug smugglers, including Chinese, Thais, Pakistanis, Indians, Iranians,

Afghans, Nigerians, and Israelis." Robert Stutman, a special agent for the FBI, noted that "these groups are posing a major challenge to law enforcement. We now are dealing with languages and cultures that we have no real depth in."

Until the federal government is willing to secure our borders, and fulfill its obligations under Article IV, Section 4 of the U.S. Constitution to "protect each State against invasion," there is little hope that the "war on drugs" can be won.

The alien-related crime that plagues this country is one of the consequences of failure to enact and enforce sensible immigration controls. The problem posed by alien criminals is not new. Since the early days of the Republic, foreign criminal elements have viewed this as a "land of opportunity."

In past years, our elected representatives passed laws to try to keep criminals out, and then enforced those statutes. But our current leaders lack the courage to deal forthrightly with this issue.

Few communities in America have gone untouched by alien-related crime. As Professor James O'Kane of Drew University observes:

> *Ethnic organized crime among current minority newcomers is flourishing and ever-expanding, with no end in sight. At a time when FBI and Department of Justice offensives against Italian organized crime are beginning to bear fruit, new ethnic mobs appear to fill the vacuum. Police and organized crime task forces scarcely know what to do about these new groups and have their hands full merely trying to describe these activities, let alone control them. With respect to certain groups (e.g. Chinese, Japanese, Vietnamese, and Soviet Jews), police even lack undercover agents who speak the same language as the newcomer criminals!*
> *The prognosis for the elimination of ethnic*

organized crime is indeed grim. Compounding this reality is an equally depressing one: many of the former lower-income ethnic criminals have not necessarily become law-abiding citizens. Many simply have "moved up" to white-collar crime, and as such, have blended with the dominant groups in American life ...[23]

Professor O'Kane tells us that we constantly delude ourselves into thinking that ethnic crime is "on the way out."

An Invitation to Terrorists

Another related issue is terrorism. Until last year, the worst acts of terrorism around the world had not occurred on American territory. But in 1993, two extraordinary incidents reminded us that terrorists are here who bear malice toward the U.S. and its citizens:

• The assassination of two CIA employees, and wounding of three more, at the entrance gate of the Agency's headquarters in McLean, Virginia, on January 25, 1993. The suspected gunman, Mir Aimal Kansi, a 29-year old Pakistani who had asked for "asylum." Kansi remains at large.

• The bombing of the World Trade Center by Islamic terrorists who had likewise been permitted to stay in this country after petitioning for "asylum."

Our poorly-guarded borders and lax visa, asylee and refugee policies provide inviting opportunities for terrorists, as well as other criminals.

Conclusion

The INS' main enforcement unit in the interior, the Investigations Division, is responsible for the following broad categories: criminal aliens (including criminal organizations and terrorist deportation cases); fraud (including false or fraudulently-obtained documents, as well as visa, asylum, and marriage fraud); anti-smuggling activities; maintenance of the INS Violent Gang Task Force, which cooperates with other law enforcement agencies dealing with ethnic gang-related problems in major metropolitan areas; and participation in the federal Organized Crime Drug Enforcement Task Forces; as well as administering Employer Sanctions.

The Investigations Division has only 1,650 employees, called "special agents," to contend with the hundreds of thousands of aliens who engage in violent criminal activities (in 1990, federal, state, and local authorities arrested 226,080 foreign-born individuals for "aggravated felonies"). By contrast, there are approximately 1,200 Capitol Police to patrol an area measured in city blocks.

To be effective, control of criminal and terrorist activities committed by aliens must be comprehensive and balanced. Border security, airport and seaport inspections, and interior enforcement are complimentary functions. It is critical that both the INS Investigations Division and the Border Patrol be given the resources they require.[24]

Despite a pledge to crack down on the entry of alien criminals and terrorists the Clinton Administration, effective April 1,1994, ordered the INS to stop conducting routine fingerprint checks on immigrants, a procedure that has screened out thousands of would-be immigrants with criminal records in recent years. In 1993, nearly 890,000 sets of fingerprints were forwarded to the FBI by the INS and 9,000 criminals were denied legal entry. Attorney General Janet Reno said that halting the fingerprint checks would save $3 million this fiscal year.[25]

In the area of law enforcement, our immigration policy should be to do everything practical to keep criminal aliens out of the country and to deport them once they are caught.

CHAPTER FIVE
THE ENVIRONMENT AND QUALITY OF LIFE

We will not recite the full litany of environmental ills that face our country — you are no doubt more than familiar with them. We do, however, contend that virtually all are related to the size of our population, and that further growth of the U.S. population will multiply them.

Immigration fits into the equation not because immigrants consume much differently than the rest of us, but precisely because they are similar. They drive cars, heat their houses and take out the trash just like we do. One of the most common reasons people give for immigrating is to improve their standard of living — that is, increase their consumption.

Immigration is part of the environmental problem because it contributes to the size of our population, the multiplier for our environmental difficulties.

Immigration's Role in U.S. Population Growth

According to demographer Leon Bouvier, immigrants and their descendants born here accounted for just over half of the U.S. population growth of 48 million between 1970-1990.[1] Startling as that statistic is, the U.S. Census Bureau had even greater surprises in store.

Back in 1989, the Bureau had projected our population would grow slowly in the 21st century, peaking in 2050 at about 302 million (in 1990, it was 250 million). They theorized that immigration would be controlled and that low birth rates would prevail across all social, economic, racial, and ethnic groups.

By 1992, those assumptions were out the window. Thanks to Congress's increasing immigration by 40 percent in 1990, and to rising birth rates in all groups (chiefly other than what the Census Bureau calls non-Hispanic whites), they then projected a population in 2050 of 383 million, 80 million more than just 4 years earlier, and that it would continue to grow rapidly! As the *Detroit Free Press* commented, "80 million people more or less could have a huge impact on every city, transportation system, commuter, school kid..."[2] A few months later, the Census Bureau increased this estimate to 392 million.[3]

The Role of Numbers

To consider the multiplier effect of population size, and of further population growth, let us examine the case of air pollution from automobiles. To keep the mathematics simple, assume that the average automobile, driven the average number of miles, emits one hundred pounds of air pollutants per year. With one hundred such cars we have the formula:

(100 pounds per car) x (100 cars) = 10,000 pounds per year.

Now suppose that we undertake a vigorous campaign to reduce the pollutants emitted per car by requiring catalytic converters, better fuel efficiency for new cars, and so on. The average number of miles driven per auto stays the same. The program proves very successful, and as new cars gradually replace the old ones, the pounds of pollutants emitted per automobile fall until the level stands at 80 percent of what it was originally. That would certainly be a major accomplishment.

But let us further assume that during the time it takes to bring these more efficient cars on line and gradually replace the older cars in the automobile fleet, the human population, and with it the number of vehicles, increases 25 percent.

Here is our new formula:

(80 pounds per car) x (125 cars) = 10,000 pounds per year.

The improved auto efficiency has been entirely offset by the further increase in the number of cars. All of the effort and expense was for naught. The total impact on the environment is the same, and we are actually worse off than before. That is because we have used up a number of our options, and we now have even more people and cars to cope with for the next round of hoped-for improvements.

This is in fact precisely what happened in the 1980s in California, the state with the toughest anti-pollution laws for cars. The state's human population grew 25 percent from 1980 to 1990, from 24 to 30 million, but the number of registered motor vehicles actually grew 35 percent from 16,597,202 in 1980 to 22,379,770 in 1990.[4] Thus much of the improvement made in individual cars was offset by the greater number of cars on the road.

The Multiplier Effect

With the formulas above, we have illustrated the "multiplier effect" of population growth. This same dynamic applies to many resources. Gains in energy efficiency can be canceled out by an increased number of energy users. A more efficient waste water disposal plant can be overwhelmed by more people flushing their toilets. New freeways designed to relieve traffic congestion are soon overrun by an increased number of drivers. New school buildings designed to relieve crowding are soon inundated by the next wave of students. You can add to this list from your own experience.

The Tic-Tac-Toe Effect

Consider the physical effects of building more roads. In our baseline situation, let us assume four roads intersect at right angles, in the classic tic-tac-toe grid. Note that there are just four intersections:

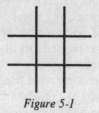

Figure 5-1

Let us double the number of roads to four running in each direction:

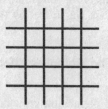

Figure 5-2

Now how many intersections are there? Not twice as many, but four times as many! If you would like a more complex and regulated life, continuing population growth is a very fine way to get there, for it increases the "intersections" we all must deal with in our daily lives.

We have tried to solve the traffic manifestation of this problem by building overpasses (which are expensive), or installing more and more traffic lights (which are vexing!). Neither alternative is pleasant.

Cases Where Increased Efficiency is NOT Possible

With problems such as air pollution, increased automobile efficiency can help neutralize the effects of population growth. But for much of what we cherish in our lives, increases in efficiency are not possible. For example, there is only so much Pacific Ocean beach in Oregon. No more is being made, and doubling the population will reduce the per capita beach front by one-half.

The same is true of our wilderness and natural areas. In some of our national parks, one must now make reservations well in advance to obtain an entry permit. Many of these areas are now being "loved to death." What will it be like if our population increases another 60 percent by 2050? We are not going to make any new Yosemites or Yellowstones.

Population Growth and Personal Liberty

In the days of the frontier (which the Census Bureau once defined as a line where the population has reached a density of two persons per square mile), individuals could do pretty much as they pleased. Part of the lore of Daniel Boone is that when he could see the smoke of another cabin, things were getting too crowded and he headed west. The frontier provided an escape valve for society's individualists and misfits, for the people who could not stand the strain of living too close to their neighbors.

There is an old saying that the freedom to swing your fist stops at the end of *my* nose. Back in the days when noses were few and far between, that was not much of a limitation.

Today, in a country like Holland, where population has reached 1300 people per square mile, this concept is very much a factor. If society is to function peaceably, everything must be agreed to, and all permits obtained in advance. The scope for the individual shrinks accordingly.

Consider the analogy of a five-gallon can. Suppose we close the lid and pump it up to twice atmospheric pressure. The walls must be of a certain strength to contain the air. If we then double the pressure again, the walls must be even stronger — if the can is not to burst. The strength of the walls required to contain the air is roughly analogous to the number of laws, rules, and regulations that we must subject ourselves to as population pressure rises.[5]

Increasing Diversity

The increasing diversity of the United States is a complex subject. Most discussions of diversity in the United States praise its virtues. Very few persons are willing to call attention to its adverse effects for fear of being labeled "racist."

Whatever the benefits of increased diversity may be, there is one unavoidable defect — it reduces that which is commonly agreed upon and taken for granted. As a result, it increases the need for laws and regulations to mediate our increasing differences. Freedom suffers accordingly.

The Cultural Defense

Cultural practices in some countries differ markedly from those in the United States. For instance, female circumcision (removal of the clitoris) is a common practice in parts of Africa. In DeKalb County, Georgia, a Somali woman was brought to trial for allegedly performing this operation on her two-year old niece. The defense: this was customary back home!

In 1989, a Chinese immigrant in New York City, Dong Lu Chen, hammered his wife to death because he suspected her of cheating on him. People were outraged when his sentence was only five years' probation. The judge relied on an anthropologist's testimony about the seriousness of infidelity in Chinese culture and on the defense's contention that shame pushed Chen to an extreme act.[6]

The "cultural defense" is appearing more frequently. Given the nature of our court system, it will probably gain acceptance as it is used more and more. Our common set of values will suffer accordingly.

Political Apathy

Every election time, we hear complaints about how few Americans vote, and how political participation is decreasing. There are doubtless many reasons for this, but one of them surely is the realistic assessment on the part of many voters that, in a constantly growing country, the individual voter counts for less and less. At some point, many realistically wonder: What is the use of voting?

In Abraham Lincoln's day, each Congressman had a constituency of about 185,000 persons. Today it is 550,000 persons. If U.S. population doubles, as the U.S. Census Bureau now predicts it will (thanks largely to immigration), the individual voter would be literally one in a million, with a correspondingly lesser chance of being heard by our federal representatives and of influencing the course of events. Giving up on the political system would doubtless become an even more common response: Why bother?

Recognizing this problem, some have even proposed expanding the size of Congress to as many as 2,000 representatives. May the saints preserve us from that!

Aesthetics and the Spiritual Life

Both authors of this book live in one of the rural, less densely populated parts of Michigan. As a result, we both make less money than our urban colleagues. But, as they say in our home town of Petoskey, located on the shores of Little Traverse Bay off Lake Michigan, "A view of the bay / Is part of the pay!"

In exchange for less money, we are able to do such things as leave home without locking our doors. We know our neighbors, and we look out for one another. We have a built-in "neighborhood watch" — no window signs are needed. We can park free all day within two blocks of our office, and have the option of walking or biking to work.

In our small-scale, socio-political situation, problems are of manageable size. A motivated individual can actually make a difference. As a result, we have a vigorous community life — people think it worthwhile to attempt improvements.

Many folks here are at least partially self-reliant, growing some of their own food, cutting their own wood for fuel. Thanks to a relatively sparse population the night sky is not yet obliterated by lights. We can still see the stars and watch the planets. These are things that define our vision of a high quality of life, things that add a spiritual and aesthetic dimension.

We are well aware that most of our readers must live in urban areas, where life is different from that described above. If reports can be believed, many urbanites would like to become ex-urbanites and enjoy some of these same pleasures. We would like to keep that option open for them, but continued population growth, now substantially fueled by immigration, stands in the way.

Summary

Edward Abbey perhaps said it best in his book *Abbey's Road*:

America offers what may be our final opportunity to save a useful sample of the original land. It is not a question merely of preserving forests and rivers, ... but also of keeping alive a certain way of human life, a wholesome and reasonable balance between industrialism and agrarianism, between cities and small towns, between private property and public property. Here it is still possible to enjoy the advantages of contemporary technological culture without having to endure the overcrowding and stress characteristic of this culture in less fortunate regions. ... [P]erhaps in the decades to come we can ... restore to all citizens of our nation their rightful heritage of breathable air, drinkable water, open space, family-farm agriculture, a truly democratic political economy. Why settle for anything less? ... [W]e may succeed in making America ... an example to other nations of what is possible and beautiful. Was that not, after all, the whole point and purpose of the American adventure?[7]

PART TWO
HOW DID WE GET INTO THIS PREDICAMENT?

CHAPTER SIX
A BRIEF HISTORY OF U.S. IMMIGRATION
AND IMMIGRATION CONTROL POLICIES
THROUGH 1952

Few topics are so obscured by layers of entrenched myth as is our immigration history. When President John Kennedy said, "We are a nation of immigrants," he failed to note that virtually every other country is as well.

America could afford to welcome people to its shores while it still enjoyed a superabundance of fertile soil and seemingly unlimited natural resources. But even in Colonial times, we did not encourage indiscriminate immigration — let alone the settlement of what Emma Lazarus' poem, now appended to the pedestal of the Statue of Liberty, describes as the world's "wretched refuse."[1]

Furthermore, just because millions of people from around the globe were able to migrate here in the past does not mean that the United States must admit relentless new waves of immigrants, forever and without limit.

Asians were the first immigrants to this continent, arriving in North America from Siberia. They are now referred to as Native Americans.[2]

European colonization of North America began in the early seventeenth century at a time when England was experiencing remarkable social and religious upheavals.[3]

The Church of England was at war with various dissenters, agricultural interests vied with nascent capitalists for economic leadership, and the aristocracy was forced to deal with demands for the extension of representative government.

For many, changes did not come quickly enough. For others, the reforms did little to improve their lot in a country that was already densely populated.

The American (and Australian) colonies proved a convenient outlet for the ambitious and the discontented.

The first permanent English settlement was established at Jamestown, Virginia, in 1607. Thirteen years later, the Pilgrims landed at Plymouth, Massachusetts. In 1623, the Dutch claimed Manhattan, which lay between the northern and southern English colonies. England seized this central region in 1664.

There were about 25,000 colonists living in North America in 1640. By 1660, the population had more than tripled to reach 80,000. Twenty-nine years later in 1689, it had increased 250 percent to 200,000.

The million mark was reached in about 1741. Benjamin Franklin claimed that only 80,000 immigrants had multiplied to produce these numbers. In the fifty years preceding the Revolution, 200,000 Scotch-Irish came to North America and constituted a sixth of the colonial population in 1776.

Religious refugees from the German Rhineland began to arrive in 1683. William Penn, who operated his colony both as a refuge for Quakers and as a real estate venture, sent agents to the German states to recruit Quakers and Pietists to emigrate to Pennsylvania. Thirty-thousand Germans arrived in 1708-1709, though many of them surely came as a consequence of the French occupation of their homelands in the Palatinate.

Starting in 1717, a new breed of unscrupulous entre-preneurs, known as "new-landers" and "soul stealers," lured additional thousands of German peasants to America. Agents were paid commissions by shipmasters for each emigrant. Once they arrived, the newcomers were auctioned off as indentured servants. After providing service for a term of three to five years, these redemptioners usually received fifty acres of land.

Louis XIV's revocation of the Edict of Nantes in 1685 led French Protestants to flee to North America, after they found only temporary refuge in Holland and England. These immigrants settled in South Carolina, Virginia, New York, Rhode Island, and Massachusetts, and became leaders in the professions and business life of the colonies.

From the outset of colonization, efforts were made on this side of the Atlantic to encourage the entry only of those who were likely to make a positive contribution to society.

On the other hand, it had been the practice of England, in particular, to ship what a 1663 Act of Parliament described as "rogues, vagrants, and sturdy beggars" to North America.

During the first century of English colonization, convicts were often given the choice of "transportation" to colonial plantations as an alternative to execution by hanging. How many preferred the latter alternative is not recorded!

Massachusetts, Virginia, Pennsylvania, and Maryland were among the colonies which passed laws before 1776 expelling foreign paupers, fining shipmasters who transported indigents and criminals, and laying duties on disembarked immigrants, whether or not they were criminal or destitute.

However, these initial immigration control measures had limited success. And from 1717 until the American Revolution, an estimated 50,000 criminals were sent to America from the British Isles, 20,000 of them to Maryland alone between 1750 and 1770 (admittedly, some of these convicts had been guilty of committing such mild offenses as stealing a loaf of bread).

After the Revolution

By 1776, when Independence was declared, 2,500,000 people lived in the former British colonies. Over 82 percent were of English nationality. Remarkably, even back then, the overwhelming majority of these residents was native-born descendants of native-born ancestors.

The first official Census was taken in 1790. Four million people were counted, including approximately 750,000 black slaves. A yearly average of 10,000 immigrants continued to arrive. But the native population was multiplying at an extraordinary rate — doubling about every twenty-two years.

Compare this with the United States' fastest growing region today — the West Coast. In California, the population grew between 1980 and 1990 by 25 percent, with much of this due to immigrants and their offspring. The increase was over 7 million — 50 percent more than the total population of the United States counted in the first Census.

During and after the War of Independence, many of the states continued to pass laws affecting immigration. The Continental Congress established a policy of employing only native-born citizens in the foreign service of our country. General George Washington ordered, "No man shall be appointed a sentry who is not a native of this country." The Constitutional Convention agreed that the President and Vice-President must be native-born citizens.

What the Founders Thought

Many of the founders were, in point of fact, outspokenly opposed to further immigration to the new nation — even though immigration represented a minute percentage of population growth at that time.[4]

In 1794, Washington wrote to John Adams, "My opinion with respect to immigration is, that except for useful mechanics and some particular description of men and professions, there is no use of encouragement."

He repeated this view in a letter to Sir John St. Clair: "I have no intention to invite immigrants, even if there are no restrictive acts against it. I am opposed to it altogether."

Benjamin Franklin urged that immigration be restricted and argued against proposals that the federal government offer positive inducements to immigrants. As he stated in 1787, "The only encouragements which this government holds out to strangers are such as are derived from good laws and liberty." He continued to call for restrictions on immigration and warned states against the policy pursued by some European governments of transporting criminals to this country.

Thomas Jefferson was among those who opposed immigration. He asserted that states had the right to prohibit and regulate it. In his *Notes on Virginia*, he argued that immigrants from countries governed by absolute monarchies should not be encouraged to settle here.

From 1784 to 1820, between 250,000 and 300,000 immigrants came here. They were largely from the United Kingdom and Germany, and were, for the most part, successfully assimilated. In 1820, the federal government started to collect statistics on the number of new arrivals.

Rapid population increase in Europe, the growth of industry, and the breakup of the traditional agricultural order led hundreds of thousands of people from northern and western Europe to look elsewhere for new opportunities. While only 8,385 immigrants arrived in 1820, by 1840 annual immigration reached 84,066. Between 1841 and 1860, an additional 4,311,465 immigrants settled in the U.S. Over 87 percent of them hailed from Great Britain, Ireland, and Germany.

Public Charges

During the first half of the nineteenth century, the United States was the target of numerous refugee-style boatlifts. Various European governments still attempted to ship their criminals, mental cases, and beggars to our shores. They were met, not with the "open arms" with which the Carter Administration greeted the inmates of Fidel Castro's prisons, but by batteries of state and municipal laws against them.

In the early 1830s, Maryland, Massachusetts, and New York passed acts relating to the importation of foreign criminals and paupers. In 1836, the Massachusetts legislature passed a resolution calling on the U.S. Congress to prevent the landing of paupers at our ports. The city of New York discovered, in 1837, that three-fourths of the inmates of the municipal almshouse were foreign nationals.

On January 19, 1839, an entire boatload of paupers arrived in New York City, their passage having been paid by the municipal authorities of Edinburgh, Scotland. Most were still wearing their poorhouse uniforms. Angry citizens forced the shipmasters to take the unwelcome passengers back to Scotland and to reimburse the city of New York for the expenses incurred on their account.

At the request of the U.S. House and Senate, the Secretary of State and Secretary of the Treasury collected what information could be obtained concerning the deportation of paupers and criminals from Europe. In 1837, the U.S. consulate in Leipzig, Germany, reported:

> *Not only paupers, but even criminals, are transported from the interior of the country to the sea-ports in order to be embarked there for the United States. A Mr. De Stein has lately made propositions to the smaller cities of Saxony for transporting their criminals to the port of Bremen, and embarking them there for the United States at $75 per head, which offer has been accepted by several of them. ... It has of late, also, become a general practice in the towns and boroughs of Germany, to get rid of their paupers and vicious members, by collecting means for effectuating their passage to the United States.*

Despite official protests, the practice continued. In 1855, the government of the Kingdom of Wurttemberg denied the right of the U.S. to return paupers and criminals who had been refused entry and tried to take steps to prevent their transport back to Germany. As late as 1884-1885, thousands of Irish paupers were shipped to the United States and Canada. Their passage was paid for by their government.

The Supreme Court Takes Control

The California Gold Rush stimulated the importation of Chinese workers. From 1854 to 1882, some 220,000 Chinese were admitted to this country. American workingmen saw their wages and job prospects undercut by poorly paid Chinese who were brought to this country by "cost conscious" employers.

State legislatures reacted to the influx of Chinese laborers by enacting laws to exclude them from the labor market. But in 1875, the U.S. Supreme Court ruled that all state laws regulating immigration unconstitutionally restrained interstate commerce. In response, Congress passed the first of the Chinese Exclusion Acts, which significantly reduced immigration from the Orient.

In 1882, with over 50 million people living in the United States, 788,992 legal immigrants were admitted. That same year, Congress passed the first comprehensive immigration law, which imposed a federal head tax of 50 cents on every arriving passenger from a foreign country. No ceiling was placed on the numbers permitted to come, but the principle of individual (as opposed to group) selection was made the basis of federal legislation. The aim was to exclude individual immigrants who were most likely to become a burden on society: paupers, criminals, and those afflicted with various diseases. The Secretary of the Treasury was responsible for enforcing our immigration laws, with state boards conducting an actual examination of each immigrant at the various ports of entry.

After economic recovery from the Panic of 1873, employers tried to break the back of organized labor by importing large numbers of foreign workers, especially from Europe. American miners were hit hard by competition from laborers recruited by employers from overseas who undercut the wages of American citizens. Congress finally reacted to this problem by passing the Alien Contract Labor Act of 1885, which prohibited the immigration of aliens under labor contracts.

Employers soon found a legal way around the intent of this law by advertising overseas that jobs were to be had at a given place in America, without an actual contract being extended. Agents were hired in foreign countries to place ads and assist workers to emigrate to the United States. Amendments to the Contract Labor Act were passed in 1887 and 1888, authorizing the Secretary of the Treasury to deport foreign workers found to have entered as contract laborers. The expense of their return was borne either by the ship owner or the employer who contracted for his services.

This act established the principle of deportation after arrival. In 1891, Congress outlawed the advertising of U.S. job openings overseas and barred passenger ship companies from encouraging immigration to this country. In addition, persons who brought aliens who were not legally entitled to enter the U.S. were made liable for a fine of up to $1,000 and/or imprisonment for a year. Any alien who became a public charge within one year after landing, from causes existing before their arrival, could be deported at the expense of the agent responsible for bringing in the alien, or if the agent could not be found, by the U.S. government.

In 1903, Congress created the Department of Commerce and Labor. The Commissioner General of Immigration was transferred to this new department from the Treasury. It is noteworthy that back then the federal immigration law was supposed to take labor and potential social costs into consideration.

Federal legislation may have discouraged the entry of certain classes of undesirable individuals, but the decade 1881-1890 witnessed the arrival of 5,246,613 immigrants — more than twice the number during any prior ten-year period.

World War I and Its Aftermath

Although the annual flow of new arrivals was marginally lower during the last decade of the nineteenth century, after 1900 the U.S. experienced the greatest surge of immigration up to that point.

From 1900 to 1914 and the outbreak of the First World War, immigration averaged over 800,000 annually. It exceeded one million in each of the years 1905, 1906, 1907, 1910, 1913, and 1914. The great majority of immigrants were from "new" sending areas, principally Russia, Poland, Austria-Hungary, Italy, Balkan countries, and Turkey.

The turn-of-the-century wave of Southern and Eastern European immigrants is often cited as "proof" of America's absorptive capacity. However, little consideration has been given to the fact that our own underprivileged, working-class citizens were forced to compete with these newcomers for jobs, housing, and social services.

Both Frederick Douglass and Booker T. Washington argued for the integration into the U.S. work force of unemployed and underemployed southern blacks rather than importing millions of additional white European workers.

In 1895, Washington implored white industrial leaders to open factory jobs to the underemployed freed slaves and their descendants. "Cast down your bucket where you are," was his memorable phrase.[5]

After the First World War, even greater numbers of Europeans moved here, despite our own high post-war levels of unemployment and a severe housing shortage. In 1920, 805,228 aliens came here. The Commissioner General of Immigration reported that 2 million aliens could be expected to arrive annually for years to come.

Public pressure mounted for a new approach that would finally reduce the number of immigrants admitted, and add simple qualitative tests for each individual immigrant.

In 1921, a stop-gap quota law was passed that, for the first time, placed quantitative limitations on immigration. This act was extended in 1922 to July 1, 1924, giving time for Congress to work out a more permanent plan for numerical restrictions. The immediate effect was to limit immigration to under 360,000 per year.

The Immigration Act of 1924 overwhelmingly passed the Congress in April and was signed by President Calvin Coolidge. This new immigration law took the place of the 1921 temporary law. Its centerpiece was a "national origins" plan that would take effect in 1929. Under it, each country was permitted to send immigrants in proportion to that nation's past contribution to the population of the United States, as of 1910. An annual quota of 153,714 was to be apportioned among the Eastern Hemisphere countries to which it applied. No numerical limit was set for the Western Hemisphere.

The Great Depression led to an even further reduction in immigration during the 1930s. The annual intake dropped below the levels allowed by the 1924 Act, averaging about 40,000 per year through 1940.

During World War II, restrictions on Asian immigration were eased slightly, out of deference to our Chinese allies, but overall, immigration remained very low. Immigration increased at the conclusion of the war, as a series of special enactments permitted the entry of refugees, displaced persons, foreign war brides, and others over and above the existing quotas.

A Congressional review of immigration policy launched in 1948 resulted in the McCarran-Walter Act of 1952. Passed over President Truman's veto, the Immigration and Nationality Act retained the national origins system, but increased the number of non-quota immigrants allowed to enter, such as immediate relatives of U.S. citizens.

Although a major purpose of the 1952 Act was to limit the total number of aliens admitted annually, Congress continued to pass special legislation permitting the entry of large numbers of refugees. From 1945 to 1960, over a million refugees came to the Golden Door of the United States.

CHAPTER SEVEN
THE OPENING OF THE FLOODGATES:
IMMIGRATION POLICY AFTER 1952

The change began slowly, imperceptibly — revision to an existing law here; a change in the regulations there.

Over the next three decades, it gathered momentum, moving like the great North American glaciers of the Ice Age, ever so slowly, but with a force that has created a social divide greater than our geographical Continental Divide.

The 1965 Act

The year was 1965. President Lyndon B. Johnson had just beaten Senator Barry Goldwater in what, up until that time, had been the most one-sided election in history — sweeping in the "Great Society" Congress.

It was the height of the Civil Rights Era. And in the prevailing optimism of the time, it would have been difficult for all but the most astute legislators to foresee the disastrous effects of the legislation they were about to enact.

The legislation was an immigration bill: a revision of our immigration laws that was aimed at eliminating our immigration system's traditional tilt toward Europeans. In addition, this revision of immigration law was designed to shift the selection preference from applicants with special skills to family members of those already here. The legislation went forward with little opposition and was signed into law — at a ceremony at the Statue of Liberty — just twelve weeks after it was introduced.

Specifically, the 1965 Immigration Act provided that as of July 1, 1968, every year the U.S. government would make

available 120,000 visas to persons born in the Western
Hemisphere. This was the first time limits were placed on
immigration from the Western Hemisphere. Another 170,000
visas were allotted to persons born in Eastern Hemisphere
countries, with a limit of 20,000 per country.

In language that today would be condemned for its
insensitivity, proponents of the 1965 Immigration Act promised
that the revisions would be largely symbolic and would not
result in a flood of immigrants from the Third World.

Attorney General Nicholas Katzenbach testified that no
more than 5,000 Asians were likely to immigrate to this
country in any given year.

Congressman Emanuel Celler (D-NY) certified that,
"There will not be comparatively many Asians or Africans
entering this country."[1]

Senator Robert F. Kennedy (D-NY) went even further,
assuring the House Subcommittee on Immigration that "For the
Asia-Pacific Triangle [immigration under the new act] would
be approximately 5,000, Mr. Chairman, after which
immigration from that source would virtually disappear."

His brother, Senator Edward M. Kennedy, made this
statement in favor of the new law:

> What this bill will not do: First, our cities will not be
> flooded with a million immigrants annually. Secondly,
> the ethnic mix of this country will not be upset. ...
> Contrary to the charges in some quarters, S.500 will
> not inundate America with immigrants from any one
> country or area, or the most populated and
> economically deprived nations of Africa and Asia.[2]

Nearly thirty years later, Peter Brimelow, senior editor at
Forbes, wrote, "Every one of these assurances [of the proponents of the 1965 Act] has proved false. Immigration levels did
surge upward — they are now running at a million a year."

"Immigrants *do* come predominantly from one sort of area — 85 percent of the 11.8 million legal immigrants arriving in the U.S. between 1971 and 1990 were from the Third World, 44 percent from Latin America and the Caribbean, 36 percent from Asia — *and* from one country: 20 percent from Mexico."[3]

The hidden loophole primarily responsible for this phenomenon was that immigrants could bring in relatives outside of the limits set by the 1965 Act. This not only vastly increased the number of immigrants admitted, but also created chains of migration from the same regions — brothers and sisters could bring in spouses, who in turn could bring in *their* siblings and parents and so on. This loophole remains open today.

On its face, the new law had the appearance of making immigration more accessible to immigrants of all continents. However, contrary to what its sponsors pledged, the law did not actually end preferences based on national origin.

What it did accomplish, as Senator Sam Ervin, Jr. predicted it would, was to discriminate against our traditional immigrant groups in favor of natives of the Third World.

As Theodore H. White (no foe of Lyndon Johnson and most of his works) observed in his book, *America in Search of Itself* (1982), the 1965 Immigration Act was "probably the most thoughtless of the many acts of the Great Society." He predicted that the 1965 Immigration Act would likely end up being a prime factor in "what could become a catastrophe — the tide of immigration legal and illegal, pouring into this country."

"... the United States has lost one of the cardinal attributes of sovereignty — it no longer controls its own borders. Its immigration laws are flouted by aliens and citizens alike, as no system of laws has been flouted since Prohibition."

The 1980 Refugee Act

In the spring of 1980, Congress passed the Refugee Act. The law was an outgrowth of America's post-Vietnam guilt. It was supposed to provide refuge for people unable to live in safety in their homelands and in genuine need of a safe haven.

The Act accepted the United Nations' refugee definition: "persons ... unwilling or unable to return to their country because of persecution [not *prosecution*] or a well-founded fear of persecution on account of race, religion, nationality, membership in a particular social group, or political opinion." The 1980 Refugee Act sets forth admirable goals on its surface; in fact, it left the door wide open to fraud and abuse.

Less than two months after Congress passed the Refugee Act, 125,000 Cubans, including many criminals and insane asylum inmates, were released by Cuban dictator Fidel Castro. They embarked for the U.S. in a huge flotilla of small boats. Since they did not fit into any defined refugee category, President Jimmy Carter designated them "special entrants" and welcomed them with "open arms" instead of returning them to Cuba as the law demanded.

Carter, like so many presidents before and since, used immigration for political purposes. Finding himself in an election year, he did not want to offend the powerful Cuban-American voting bloc, which held the balance of power in Florida politics. As Jack Watson, Carter's assistant for Intergovernmental Affairs, explained, "We decided that it would be counter-productive to enforce the laws."[4] President Ronald Reagan later granted them refugee status.

Other Subtle Abuses

For example, the 1980 Refugee Act did not address a seldom-used loophole in the law: asylum. Under asylum provisions a person seeks protection after having entered the

U.S. Prior to 1980, fewer than 5,000 persons applied annually for asylum. Since an asylum claim stays deportation proceedings, it has become a popular instrument to avert deportation and remain in this country. Asylum adjudications often take years to complete.

In addition, aliens are routinely granted permission to work while their cases are undergoing review. Some marry Americans, gaining by this means the right to stay permanently. Furthermore, there are no limits to the number of persons who may be granted asylum in a given year.

Economic Refugees

Nowhere in the 1980 Refugee Act is it stated that those fleeing adverse economic conditions (the primary reason for most of the world's emigration) should be granted asylum or refugee status, either individually or wholesale. Yet time and again Congress has made exceptions. Congress made up a special category of refugees for Salvadorans, enabling 17 percent of that country's population to remain in our country indefinitely.

In a major omission, the 1980 Refugee Act doesn't require our government to seek the cooperation of other nations in the resettlement of truly persecuted refugees. Congress also set no firm limits on refugee admissions, leaving the President to establish an admissions number annually after *pro forma* "consultation with Congress." As a consequence, today the United States accepts more refugees for permanent resettlement than the rest of the world combined, and more than twice the 50,000 base number set in the Act.

In 1980, there were 8 million refugees officially recognized by the United Nations High Commissioner for Refugees. Today there are more than 17 million. Additional tens of millions are displaced within their own countries. Most refugees would like to settle in the United States.

The 1986 Immigration Reform and Control Act

During the Carter Administration, a blue ribbon commission led by Father Theodore Hesburgh, former president of Notre Dame, studied the growing immigration crisis. It was known as the Select Commission on Immigration and Refugee Policy.

Its basic conclusion was that immigration *must* be controlled. Its recommendations were summed up in the Introduction of the Commission's final report to Congress:

> *We recommend closing the back door to undocumented/illegal migration, opening the front door a little more to accommodate legal migration in the interests of this country, defining our immigration goals clearly and providing a structure to implement them effectively, and setting forth procedures which will lead to fair and efficient adjudication and administration of U.S. Immigration laws.*

It took Congress five years to implement any of the recommendations of the Hesburgh Commission, and Congress has yet to define our immigration goals clearly. Immigration bills passed the Senate in 1982 and 1984, only to die in the House. Finally, after years of debate, Congress passed the Immigration Reform and Control Act (IRCA) in 1986.

Employer Sanctions

IRCA was touted as a measure to control illegal immigration. Its highlight was employer sanctions — a provision that subjects employers who knowingly hire illegal aliens to civil and criminal penalties. This provision was designed so that it would help eliminate or alleviate the magnet of jobs drawing illegals here.

Fines under employer sanctions were set at $250 to $10,000 per illegal alien knowingly hired. And for the first time ever, employers were required to verify the legal status of prospective employees to assure they were entitled to a job. Proponents of immigration restriction hailed this as a very positive step forward. However, as is so often the case with immigration reform, a step forward was accompanied by two steps backward.

One of the ways Congress hobbled immigration control was to prohibit the Immigration and Naturalization Service from visiting open farm fields to question laborers about their immigration status unless they first obtained a search warrant. This has virtually ended apprehensions of illegals in such areas.

But perhaps most destructive was what Congress did not do: appropriate the funds necessary for the Immigration and Naturalization Service to enforce employer sanctions and other immigration control measures.

Amnesty

Furthermore, the price paid for employer sanctions was a terrible political trade-off: a large-scale amnesty program for illegal aliens who could prove that they had been in the U.S. since January 1, 1982. Congress pardoned millions of illegal aliens and put them on a path to citizenship. Amnesty was the political compromise required to pass employer sanctions, even though it rewarded illegal aliens who had broken our laws and entered the U.S. illegally.

The amnesty program granted "temporary resident" status to persons who illegally entered the U.S. before January 1, 1982, or who became illegal by remaining here after expiration of their temporary visas (such as those issued to students or tourists). Illegal aliens who claimed to have arrived in the U.S. before that date were given one year, from May 5, 1987, to apply for amnesty.

After 18 months of temporary resident status, amnestied aliens were permitted to become permanent residents. They were then able to apply for full citizenship after having been a permanent resident for five years (in 1993 for many of them), after which time they are eligible to petition for admission of their relatives.

In addition, Congress created a special amnesty for Cubans and Haitians who illegally entered the U.S. before January 1, 1982. Those who registered with the INS were given *immediate* permanent resident status, retroactive to 1982. Permanent resident status makes a person eligible for social service benefits. By retroactively granting these illegal aliens from the Caribbean permanent resident status, Congress made it possible for them to immediately apply for citizenship, and then start bringing in relatives.

A third special agricultural amnesty program was also included in the package, at the insistence of the powerful Western agricultural lobby. Under the Special Agricultural Worker (SAW) provisions, illegal aliens who claimed to have worked in agriculture in the U.S. for 90 days during the 12-month period from May 1, 1985, to May 1, 1986, were allowed to apply for temporary resident status. Those who claimed to have been in the U.S. since January 1, 1982, were eligible to apply for permanent resident status.

This triggered another surge in illegal immigration. People from around the world, many of whom never spent a day picking crops in the U.S., applied for amnesty under this provision. There were applicants who testified that they had harvested baked beans, or picked strawberries from stepladders! Some farmers sold affidavits for hundreds of dollars each to aliens, certifying that the individual had been employed on their farm at the appropriate time.

One woman from New Jersey, who owned a five-acre garden plot, certified that over 1,000 illegal aliens had worked for her.

Some aliens in New York City, Queens, and Manhattan, stated on their amnesty applications that they had picked watermelons for a Texas rancher. Few had ever been to Texas, much less worked in agriculture. Many turned out to be well-educated professionals.

Another example of this fraud was the recent 17-count indictment on April 5, 1994, filed against Jose Velez, national president of the League of United Latin American Citizens (LULAC), and three Taiwanese, Billy Tzeng, Al Feng, and Simon Chang, for running an "assembly line" operation that provided wealthy Asians with fraudulent documents to enable them to apply for amnesty. False work records indicating that they had been living in the U.S. before 1982, or that they had been farm workers entitled to SAW provisions, were issued for fees ranging from a few hundred dollars to as much as $45,000.

On March 22, 1994, Velez's son, Peter, pleaded guilty to assisting his father's immigration fraud business that processed 5,600 false applications for nearly $5.7 million.[5]

Sponsors of the SAW program publicly stated that only 350,000 people would apply for amnesty under its provisions. In Arizona, amnesty applications were five times greater than the number of all farm worker jobs in the state! In the end, over 1.2 million people — nearly three times the number needed to pick *all* our perishable crops — applied for SAW amnesty.

The total number of aliens who took advantage of the amnesty programs of the 1986 Act was over 3.1 million.

Results

Yet in spite of its tremendous shortcomings, IRCA temporarily reduced the flow of illegal aliens into the United States. News of the new law was reported throughout the world. In Mexico, it received a great deal of attention from the press.

However, Congressional opponents of immigration limitation soon subverted the spirit of the new law by derailing increased appropriations for the INS, including a promised 50 percent increase in Border Patrol personnel. The money actually made available was not enough to fund the expanded duties assigned to the INS, including the enforcement of employer sanctions and expanded participation in the War on Drugs, which are largely functions of the INS Investigations Division.

The decline in illegal immigration was short-lived. Would-be immigrants quickly discovered new ways to gain access to the U.S. using fraudulent documents.

Document Fraud

In the wake of the 1986 Act, a network of mills counterfeiting documents has emerged — leading Father Hesburgh, former chairman of the Select Commission on Immigration and Refugee Policy, to describe the U.S. as a "document forger's paradise." As long as government agencies refuse to issue tamper-resistant birth certificates, driver's licenses, and Social Security cards, document fraud will remain a major obstacle to effective immigration law enforcement.

Finally, under IRCA, the federal government was to reimburse states for welfare, health, and education services provided to amnestied aliens. But the $1 billion annual appropriation lasted for only four years and failed to cover many state and local government costs.

The 1990 Immigration Act

On November 29, 1990, President George Bush signed another new immigration act. In response to claims that the nation faced a looming "labor shortage," the annual immigration ceiling was raised from 530,000 to 700,000 through February, 1994, and 675,000 thereafter, thus expanding legal immigration by almost 40 percent.

From these totals, 140,000 visas were reserved for immigrants holding "special skills." Ten thousand visas were set aside for wealthy individuals who promised to invest at least $500,000 in businesses that might create new jobs.

Senator Edward M. Kennedy insisted on the provision of 40,000 visas a year for Europeans, including a minimum of 16,000 for Irish immigrants, taking us back toward the "national origins" system that Kennedy had fought against in the 1965 Immigration Act! Special "temporary protected status" was granted to Salvadorans until June, 1992. Hostilities in El Salvador have ceased, yet the Salvadorans have not been sent home.

Communists and many other formerly excluded classes are no longer prohibited from entering our country, a boon to former oppressors fleeing the onset of democracy in the former Soviet Union and East Bloc.

Meanwhile, as all these changes in laws, policy, and regulations caused the numbers of immigrants to soar, other political changes slowed down absorption, assimilation, and Americanization of those already here — a process that had characterized every previous wave of immigration.

CHAPTER EIGHT
THE WORLD COMES TO THE U.S.

Immigration now accounts for a larger percentage of U.S. population growth than ever before in our history. From 1970-1990 immigrants and the children they had *after arriving here* accounted for slightly more than half of our population growth of 50 million.

As a result of the 1990 Immigration Act and other legislation, over a million legal immigrants, asylees and refugees were admitted in 1992. In addition, an unknown number of people entered illegally with the intention of staying permanently. The Border Patrol estimates that for each of the 1.25 million-plus apprehensions made in 1993, as many as two persons more made it in undetected. (How many of the legal and illegal entrants eventually return home is not known either, since the INS stopped keeping track of emigration in 1957.)

These growing numbers of immigrants, both legal and illegal, far outstrip immigration at the turn of the century, long viewed as the high-water mark of U.S. immigration. This is true both in absolute numbers and as a percentage of our population growth.

I. ILLEGAL IMMIGRATION

Proponents of the 1986 Immigration Reform and Control Act (IRCA) promised that this measure would stem the flood of illegal aliens. The year before the Act was passed, the Border Patrol apprehended 1.76 million people entering our country illegally.

At first, it appeared that IRCA would have a positive effect. Following its passage, the number of aliens apprehended along our southern border dropped. Federal agencies pledged to "get tough" and enforce employer sanctions provisions making it more difficult for illegal entrants to obtain employment.

After the law came into effect, highly publicized raids on a few select businesses that employed large numbers of illegal aliens gave the impression that the U.S. government was finally cracking down. The virulently anti-American Mexican press inadvertently contributed to the initial effectiveness of IRCA by publishing sensational stories charging that the new law was "racist" and was fostering the indiscriminate arrest of Hispanics.

The respite was relatively short-lived. Arrests at San Diego — the prime entry area — set new records in January and February, 1988, (up 13 percent over January, 1987, and 24 percent over February, 1987). This pattern has continued.

As early as December, 1987, the U.S. Embassy in El Salvador reported that "illegal migration to the United States is increasing and has risen back to 1984-86 levels." By 1985, over 10 percent of El Salvador's population was living in the United States, chiefly in California, and tens of thousands more have come since then. The Embassy study noted that Salvadorans were convinced "that the United States is not serious about enforcing its immigration law. ... So-called travel agencies engaged in smuggling Salvadorans into the United States report that business has returned to normal after a sharp decline in the months after passage of the immigration law."

The State Department was alerted by our embassy that there would be "an astronomical increase" in applications for visas throughout the rest of the decade and into the 1990s as Salvadorans apply to join relatives amnestied by the 1986 IRCA. Ernesto Rivas-Gallont, Salvadoran ambassador to the

United States, confirmed the validity of the assessment: "Immigration, legal and illegal, from El Salvador to the United States has not really decreased."

Overall, the Border Patrol apprehended 1.10 million illegal aliens in the twelve-month period ending September 30, 1990, and 1.13 million during the following twelve months. During 1993, they apprehended 1.25 million illegal aliens, an increase of about 4.4 percent over 1992. Roughly half were caught in the San Diego sector.

As immigration researcher Doris Meissner (now INS Commissioner) explained, "There is evidence that many potential immigrants waited for a while to see how the law worked and have since begun moving again."

The Role of Population Pressure

To put the effectiveness of the 1986 Act in the proper perspective we need to emphasize that during the seven years since it passed, world population has been increasing by 90-plus million per year, for a total addition of about 600 million people — more than twice the entire U.S. population. Ninety percent of these people are born in the less-developed countries, so the population pressure on the U.S. immigration system has increased markedly — by about 15 percent. Any fixed solution, such as the 1986 Immigration Act, applied to a growing problem like population will necessarily become obsolete very quickly.

New Migrant Networks

As the march of immigrants accelerated, new networks were established to channel people in from parts of Mexico that were not significant sources of illegal aliens in the past. Wayne Cornelius, director of the Center for U.S.-Mexican Studies at the University of California at San Diego, conducted a field expedition to Mexico, and discovered many communities that sent migrant workers to the U.S. had become "virtual ghost towns."

In California, he interviewed some of the newly arrived illegal aliens and was told they were determined to remain in the U.S., notwithstanding fear of arrest by federal immigration authorities. Their view was summed up by one illegal alien, who said, "We will stay until the *migra* [the Border Patrol] takes us out, and afterward we will return here again."

Investigations carried out in Mexico, California, and Texas confirm that first-time illegal entry is increasing. Traffic is no longer seasonal. Border Patrol agents are now making record numbers of arrests even during the winter months, formerly the slow period.

Another disturbing trend: many illegal aliens are coming as family units. Previously, mostly single males came for short term work and then returned home. Now entire families are migrating. Most have no intention of returning home unless they are sent back.[1]

The Trampoline

In addition to hundreds of thousands of illegals pouring in from Latin America, Mexico has become a "trampoline" for increasing numbers of people from around the world. Natives of Albania, China, Yugoslavia, Poland, Turkey, Ghana, Pakistan, and India are among those crossing into the U.S. through Mexico. Said Duke Austin of the INS, "The word is out all over the world that if you can make it to Mexico, you stand a good chance of getting into the United States."

Few illegals try to cross over by themselves. Most hire a professional smuggler, commonly known as a "coyote." For $200 or more a head, coyotes lead people in, attempting to elude the Border Patrol. After climbing over, tunnelling under, or going around or through the fence that covers a small portion of our border, they are escorted through dry river beds or canyons, or across rough hill country. Once they have collected their fee, illegal alien smugglers will often abandon their charges if there is a danger of being arrested.

In one widely publicized incident, 18 illegal aliens died after they were deserted by smugglers in a locked railroad box car in Sierra Blanca, Texas. A few days later, 19 illegal aliens were rescued from a box car in Hebbronville, Texas, while 88 illegals were pulled from a locked tractor-trailer rig at the San Clemente, California, highway checkpoint.

Coyotes will sometimes accept a down payment for a group, depositing the women and children in a safe house until the others in the party collect enough money to ransom them.

Illegal aliens are devising new tactics to gain illegal entry. Starting in late January, 1992, people from the Mexican side of the border began to sprint headlong into oncoming traffic along Interstate Highway 5 at San Ysidro, California. Coyotes organize groups numbering a hundred or more and instruct them to simply dash through the border checkpoints, dodging motorists on the American side, who sometimes cannot avoid hitting them. Aliens crossing the busy highways along the border have become a major hazard, and dozens have been killed in recent months.

A variant of this tactic is for aliens to congregate at a point along the fence dividing U.S. and Mexico. After dozens, even hundreds, assemble, they run en masse across the dry bed of the Tijuana River, in what are called "banzai charges." Even when the Border Patrol sees them coming, they lack the manpower to apprehend the vast numbers.

Illegal aliens from Mexico are usually just sent back across the border. They are then free to try again. Some are caught several times in a single night. Since most have traveled hundreds of miles to the border, recrossing is easier than returning home.

Those from other countries who are apprehended by the INS must be flown home — at U.S. taxpayer expense.

At what is known on the border as 'The Elbow' on the North Levy outside of San Ysidro, California, aliens who elude the Border Patrol at entry points frequently seek cover in a federal public housing project. In a policy continued by the Clinton Administration, President Bush's HUD Secretary, Jack Kemp, in effect made HUD projects "sanctuaries," declaring them off-limits to the INS. From the safety of a HUD project, illegal aliens then slip into the community and head for other destinations throughout the U.S.

The Border Patrol is often the least of the hazards faced by illegal aliens. Before they leave for the U.S., corrupt Mexican officials usually demand bribes. Gangs operating on the Mexican side of the border also shake down emigres.

Once across the border, they are frequently preyed upon by bandits, who are themselves often Mexicans. They steal their valuables — a cheap watch, a few dollars — and do not hesitate to rape and even kill. Locations along the U.S. side of the border are so dangerous that they have become "no man's lands" where law enforcement personnel venture at their peril. The San Diego County Sheriff's Department, in 1992, identified 17 Mexican cross-border gangs operating in their sector.

Merchandising the U.S.A.

An international immigration industry has emerged. The INS has identified 51 countries connected with alien smuggling rings, the web of transportation networks that bring would-be immigrants into the U.S.

Ads hawking the services of "immigration specialists" are published in journals reaching millions of potential customers overseas. Co-author John Tanton discovered a book, *Getting Into America*, on sale at the Hong Kong airport. *The Economist* of February 5, 1994, carried four ads in its "Business & Personal" section offering help in obtaining a U.S. immigrant visa or a second foreign passport.

Alien smugglers, operating under the cover of travel agencies, first obtain visas for their clients to travel to Mexico. Upon arrival there, clients are transported to cities across from California, Arizona, or Texas. Having paid these "travel agents" fees ranging into the tens of thousands of dollars, they then must pay "coyotes" additional hundreds of dollars to lead them into our country. Illegal aliens commonly pay "travel agents" for their services by carrying drugs across the border.

While entry into the U.S. via Mexico is preferred by most illegals, some enter from Canada, through international air terminals, and by sea. During the first half of 1993, five large freighters packed with illegal Chinese aliens were intercepted in U.S. waters. One of these, the *Golden Venture*, ran aground off the coast of Long Island. This particular episode helped publicize the extensive alien smuggling trade controlled by foreign criminal organizations.

Former Panamanian dictator Manuel Noriega used his country as a staging area for entry to the U.S. and Canada. Tens of thousands of people from Latin America and Asia paid fees of $10,000 to $20,000 each for the services of Noriega's alien-smuggling operation. When he was overthrown by the U.S. military, about 16,000 people were caught in the pipeline, including 7,000 Chinese and 3,000 Cubans (the State Department permitted the latter to enter the U.S. anyway!).

Illegal Entry Through Airports

International airports have become open doors into America. All arriving aliens need do is say the magic words "political asylum." They are then released into the U.S. "on parole" (since the INS lacks facilities to detain them) while their cases await review. The backlog of applications is so large that, on average, fourteen months lapse before a hearing is scheduled. Two-thirds of those set free ("paroled") do not show up for their asylum hearing, having long since melted into the population of an American city. Only 10 to 15 percent of those who do attend their hearings are granted asylum.

A common technique is to board flights to the U.S. with forged documents. In some cases, smugglers accompany the aliens and collect the false papers during the trip for reuse. In other instances, individuals just dispose of their documents before landing. In either instance, they arrive from Brazil, Hong Kong, Nigeria, Russia, Greece, Britain, and elsewhere, provide no documentation at all, and request asylum. Under current guidelines the INS must accept whatever name and nationality they claim.

In 1990, 43,580 aliens arrived at U.S. airports without valid travel documents, up from 19,168 in 1987. At New York City's Kennedy International Airport, the flood of illegal aliens without documents is expected to exceed 10,000 this year. Said INS district director William Slattery, "The numbers are so great now that the word is clearly out that there is a lack of a deterrent at Kennedy Airport. As such, anybody in the world who wants to come can come."

One solution to this problem is to immediately expel aliens who arrive at U.S. airports without valid documents or no passport at all, requiring the airlines to fly them back to their point of origin. Justice Department officials believe this would significantly deter those who use the long asylum backlogs and delays to gain entry.

However, the Clinton Administration has not yet submitted the required legislation to Congress, fearing opposition from "human rights" special interest groups, such as the Refugee Project of the New York Lawyers Committee for Human Rights — which has long fought the detention of asylum seekers.

People petitioning for asylum are only a portion of those who enter the U.S. through airports and do not leave. Lindsey Grant, a former Deputy Assistant Secretary of State, after checking airline manifests, discovered that "one to two million more people fly into the U.S. each year than fly out — and the number has been rising." The gap between arrivals and departures has widened from less than four million for the decade of the 1960s to nearly 16 million during the 1980s."[2] Grant points out that these missing airline passengers are not included in the annual government estimates of the number of illegal aliens who enter this country.

Marriage Fraud

Over the past six years, an annual average of 130,000 immigrants have been marrying American citizens. No one knows how many of these are fraudulent liaisons, contracted to permit aliens to enter or remain in this country. Foreigners who marry U.S. citizens obtain permanent-resident status after two years. Ninety days before their second wedding anniversary, the couple may submit a joint petition to change the alien spouse's status to permanent residency. According to the Marriage Fraud Act of 1986, if the marriage does not last for the two-year minimum, the immigrant spouse is subject to deportation.

"Lonely hearts" services connect aliens to prospective American spouses. Personal ads carried in leading magazines promise that "ladies," frequently from various parts of Asia or the former Soviet Union, "are anxious to form serious relationships" with U.S. citizens. In other cases, foreigners already here on tourist or student visas prolong their stay by marrying citizens. Not uncommonly, after the two-year waiting period, they promptly file for divorce.

Over the years, the INS Investigations Division has broken syndicates that arrange phony marriages. One such ring operating in suburban Washington, D.C., involved a number of AT&T employees who were each paid $3,000 to marry Peruvians. Another case involved a college student in Chicago, who offered to stage a sham marriage in exchange for a new motorcycle so that she could commute to classes. It is uncertain just how widespread this practice is. However, "mail-order bride" businesses, most of which involve Third World nationals, are proliferating.

Every year, of the millions who legally enter the United States with non-immigrant visas, such as students and tourists, many thousands overstay their visas. Since Congress has failed to provide the INS Investigations Division with the manpower, the technology (INS Investigations does not yet have an electronic case-tracking system) and the authority to track these "visa overstays," their numbers are unknown. In any given year, they may add 250,000 or more to the total number of illegal aliens who enter and remain here permanently.

II. LEGAL IMMIGRATION

In 1991, 1,024,000 legal immigrants settled here. In 1992, about 1,073,000 were granted legal status. (As we go to press, 1993 figures have not been released by the Justice Department.) These annual totals do not include the hundreds of thousands of illegal immigrants who will succeed in crossing our borders, many of whom stay permanently. Nor do they include asylees or refugees.

At a time when other industrialized nations are restricting immigration (in the spring of 1992, Australia cut its annual intake from 160,000 to 80,000), and despite polls confirming widespread opposition to immigration by the American public, Congress, in 1990, passed a new Immigration Act, which substantially increased legal immigration. Nearly 600,000 new immigrant job seekers will now be admitted legally every year to compete with our own unemployed, unless Congress rolls back the increases in the 1990 Act. (On average, about 55 percent of immigrants immediately enter the job market.)

The INS issued 1,103,053 work authorizations for the Fiscal Year ending September 30, 1992. Since our economy only created about 530,000 net new jobs during 1992, the work permits issued to immigrants exceeded net new jobs by as much as 600,000. And these figures do not even take into account the millions of illegal aliens who came as well.

Four noteworthy features of the 1990 Act:

First, it established a lottery for 40,000 "green cards" that grant permanent resident status, leading to eventual citizenship and the right to petition for relatives to enter. Of these, 40 percent were specifically designated for Irish applicants. No other country has ever used a lottery or any other random method to hand out the prized opportunity for citizenship.

Over 15 million applications were submitted for the coveted slots. Some individuals submitted them by the hundreds to increase their chances in the drawing. Many were posted in the United States by illegal aliens. The mail was so heavy in some post offices that it delayed regular deliveries!

Second, another provision allots 10,000 permanent resident visas annually for foreigners who pledge to invest $1 million (or $500,000 in rural or inner-city areas) and create at least ten new jobs. The foreign investor must abide by terms of the visa for only two years. How closely will this program be monitored? In Australia and New Zealand similar programs have been flagrantly abused. Once in the country, many "investors" have sent the money home to "finance" the next "investor."

Third, the 1990 Act granted a fourth amnesty, this time to the spouses and children of the 3.1 million aliens amnestied under the 1986 IRCA. We have no estimate of how many additional millions this may finally total. It will likely multiply the 3.1 million by 2 or 3 or more times, given the large size of many immigrant families. Once here, they will almost certainly have more children, so it could easily add 10 million people or more — equal to the population of the State of Michigan.

Finally, the 1990 Act granted "safe haven" for an estimated 500,000 Salvadorans illegally living in the United States. This "temporary protected status" was supposed to expire June 30, 1992. But under pressure from immigrant-rights organizations, their stay was extended one year. To date, none has yet been sent home.

Aside from the various immigration categories provided in the 1990 Act, aliens may also obtain legal status thanks to two other unique provisions of U.S. law: Congressional Private Bills and Birthright Citizenship.

Private Bills

Private Bills are an obscure avenue to legal resident alien status and then citizenship. Aliens otherwise ineligible for immigration have a member of Congress introduce a special bill granting them permanent residency. Article I of the Constitution, which grants Congress the power to "establish a uniform rule of naturalization," has been interpreted to authorize these Private Immigration Bills.

Over the years, 6,700 people have benefitted from such bills. One person who did not benefit from this procedure was U.S. Senator Harrison Williams of New Jersey who, in the ABSCAM scandal of 1980, was convicted of taking a $25,000 bribe to introduce a Private Immigration Bill.

Anchor Babies

Ratified in 1868 as a measure to protect recently freed black slaves, the 14th Amendment to the U.S. Constitution has been interpreted by the U.S. Supreme Court as granting citizenship to anyone born within the geographic limits of the U.S., even if the individual's parents are not citizens or legal residents.

Popularly known as the "citizen child loophole," this provision is used every year by thousands of illegal aliens to obtain instant citizenship for their newborns — with all of the attendant benefits available to Americans.

Along the Texas-Mexican border, people frequently use the services of *parteras* (midwives) who, for anywhere from $200 to $700, provide pregnant women with delivery care, as well as U.S. citizenship forms and supporting documentation for their infants.

"Mexicans who cannot afford American immigration lawyers after their kids are born, go to American *parteras* before their kids are born," reports Professor Margarita Tagle of Texas A&I University. According to Professor Tagle, 140 *parteras* are doing business on the U.S. side of the border between Brownsville and Laredo, Texas — about one per mile. If complications arise, women are sent to local public hospitals at U.S. taxpayer expense. For the parents, this is a grand method for gaining access to life in the U.S.[3]

In Los Angeles County alone, nearly two-thirds of the children born in county-operated hospitals during 1990-1993 were the offspring of illegal alien parents. As instant citizens, the children are entitled to health, education, and other welfare benefits, including Aid to Families with Dependent Children (AFDC). Although the parents of these new citizens are not legally entitled to benefits, welfare agencies send checks to the parents for the child's use — an obvious inducement to illegal immigration. The average monthly payment per family in California is $620 — not including Supplemental Security Income (SSI) or other benefits.

"There has been explosive growth in that area, as high as 25 percent in 1991-92, up 17 percent [in 1993]. ... It is the fastest growing area of welfare dependency in California," according to Amy Albright of the State Department of Social Services.[4] Currently, a half-million citizen-children and their illegal alien parents cost California taxpayers over $5.3 billion just for Medi-Cal, criminal incarcerations, education, and AFDC, according to Rice University economist Donald Huddle.[5]

Government authorities seldom deport illegal aliens whose children are U.S. citizens. And, upon reaching the age of 18, citizen-children may petition to legally bring in members of their family — hence the term "anchor baby," a baby that makes it possible for a whole family to gain entry to our immigration and social welfare systems.

The United States is virtually the only country that bases citizenship on the mere fact of having been born here. The overwhelming majority of other countries base it on the legal status of the parents.

A number of American legal scholars, notably Peter Schuck and Rogers Smith of Yale University, argue that the 14th Amendment's citizenship clause pertains only to the children of those legally admitted to permanent residence. Few believe that the framers of the 14th Amendment ever intended to extend citizenship to the children of illegal aliens, a concept that did not even exist in 1868.[6]

As we go to press, Representative Elton Gallegly (R-CA) has introduced two measures to close the "citizen child loophole," including a constitutional amendment that would repeal the citizenship clause of the 14th Amendment. In addition, new language would be added clarifying that automatic birthright citizenship is conferred on all persons born in this country, provided that the mother is a legal resident of the United States.

A second bill takes a statutory approach. It amends the Immigration and Nationality Act to limit citizenship at birth to persons with legal resident mothers.

III. REFUGEES AND ASYLEES

The United States has provided a safe haven for individuals genuinely subject to persecution and oppression in their native lands.

In the past, because of the country's seemingly boundless resources and open space, this rarely came under widespread scrutiny. It was easier to extend this generosity to others when we had a relatively small population in relation to the size of our country.

In 1991, and again in 1992, the U.S. admitted over 155,000 refugees and asylees. Refugees are persons living outside the U.S. who have a "well-founded fear of persecution"; asylees are persons *already in the U.S.* who claim that they will be subjected to "persecution and oppression" should they be forced to return home.

The above figures do not include people in the U.S. who have applied for asylum, but whose cases have not yet been heard. In 1991, asylum applicants numbered 56,310. The total nearly doubled in 1992 to 103,964. In 1993, 147,200 new asylum applications were filed.[7]

According to Freedom House, 41 percent of the world's population live under conditions that they describe as "not free," and another 40 percent live under "partially free" circumstances. Thus, 81 percent of the world's population of 5.4 billion could conceivably be considered potential candidates for admission to the U.S. as refugees. That comes to about 4 billion people — 16 times the current U.S. population.[8]

Soviet "Refugees"

An estimated 40 percent of the refugees who will enter the U.S. in 1994 will come from the Commonwealth of Independent States (the former Soviet Union). Over one million citizens of the former U.S.S.R. have petitioned for entry into the U.S. Some Russian officials estimate that 20 million or more wish to depart in the near future. But almost no one emigrating from the former Soviet Union fits the UN definition of a refugee. Religious persecution has ended and political expression has never been freer. Why, are so many Soviets coming to this country?

As Don Barnett, who has long been involved in Russian refugee assistance, points out, the primary lure is the American welfare state: "On any day, the main Russian emigre newspaper in New York City, *Novoye Russkoye Slovo*, is crammed with advertisements for lawyers and 'consultants' hawking advice on how to work the ropes of social services. ... Advertisements such as these are aimed at new immigrants in America and would-be immigrants in the Soviet Union still considering a move to the 'poor man's paradise.' From the perspective of the Soviet village, the deal being offered resembles an all-expenses-paid vacation to Disneyland."[9]

Israeli journalist Avishai Margalit, writing in *The New York Review of Books*, noted that much Soviet emigration to Israel is motivated by the prospect of moving on to America. "The fact that most emigrants from the former Soviet Union *can* go to Israel proves that they could not possibly be refugees as that term is normally defined," Don Barnett observes.[10]

Middle Easterners and Africans

The United States is now home to over 900,000 Arabs, almost all of whom are post-1965 arrivals and their children. In 1992, more than 27,000 Arabs entered this country, 68 percent more than ten years ago. Some are here thanks to the 1965 Immigration Act, which opened this country to massive non-Western immigration. Others have come as refugees or asylees.

Not content with security, economic opportunities, and social and political freedoms largely unknown in their homelands, Arab American leaders are now calling on Congress to designate them an official "minority" so that they can obtain "affirmative action" benefits. Said Ismael Ahmed, executive director of the Arab Community Center for Economic and Social Services in Detroit, "Arab Americans are in the same boat with other minorities in America. We share the same problems: high unemployment in urban centers, discrimination, separate cultures. We have a history of colonialism."[11]

Thanks to what has evolved into a racial spoils system at the expense of America's majority population, Arab Americans would reap many advantages from official "minority" status. At the 1994 leadership conference of the Washington, D.C.-based Arab-American Institute, which drew Commerce Secretary Ron Brown and Health and Human Services Secretary Donna Shalala as guests, community leaders claimed that they could net hundreds of millions of dollars in federal set-aside contracts. For example, if recognized by the government as a "minority" group, they could petition the Small Business Administration for Section 8(a) company contracts, which are awarded to select "minorities" without competition. During 1993, over $4 billion in federal 8(a) contracts were awarded. Omar Kader, past executive director of the American-Arab Anti-Discrimination Committee and president of Pal-Tech, told the conference, "We are subject to racial and ethnic bias. Look at the opportunities that are denied us in the business world."[12]

The U.S. is now home to the largest community of Chaldeans (Aramaic- and Arabic-speaking Roman Catholic natives of Iraq) outside of the Mideast. Over 60,000 live in metropolitan Detroit. Led by Bishop Ibrahim Mar Ibrahim, they are lobbying the Clinton Administration to take in Persian Gulf citizens currently residing in other countries, such as Turkey, Italy, Crete, and Malta.

Thus far, the State Department has resisted efforts to allow all the Chaldeans to move to the U.S., arguing that under internationally accepted standards, they are not victims of political persecution. "If we looked at it any other way, we would basically be opening up the doors to the United States. It is better to try to resolve the situations in these countries so people can go home," remarked a State Department official.

However, Edward Kennedy, chairman of the Senate Subcommittee on Refugee Affairs, is championing their cause. The United States Catholic Conference would like the U.S. to take in as many Chaldeans as wish to come here.[13]

One of the consequences of the United Nations-sponsored U.S. intervention in Somalia has been the arrival of refugees from that backward African nation. The numbers who have come, or who have petitioned for entry, have not been disclosed by the Clinton Administration.

A profile of one of the first Somalis to come here, featured in the *Chicago Tribune*, was revealing. Haji Hussein Hassan Mohamed, along with 22 of his children and one of his wives, was flown to Chicago from a refugee camp in Kenya, thanks to Lutheran Immigration and Refugee Services, at a cost of over $30,000 in airline fares alone (another wife and child were left behind "somewhere in Somalia"). Three apartments were required to house them. Reverend Stephen Swanson noted that, "they're starting from scratch. ... They come over here with all kinds of medical needs, and very few know English." Mr. Mohamed reported that his family is adjusting to life in the U.S. As for his homeland, he shrugged and said, "My mother country, I might go see it and visit it."[14]

The Rise of Islam in America

Although approximately 18 percent of the world's population are Muslims, Islam is a relatively new force in North America. An estimated four to five million Muslims currently live in the United States. Today there are over 1,000 mosques, up from 500 just fifteen years ago.

About 56 percent of the U.S. Muslim population is composed of recent immigrants. Twelve percent is of Arabic origin. A quarter is of Indo-Pakistani origin, 5 percent African, 4 percent Iranian, and there is a scattering from Turkey, and Southeast Asia. American blacks constitute 42 percent of the total.[15]

Nearly twice as many Muslims than Episcopalians live here. More Muslims live in the U.S. than in Libya. If immigration of high fertility Muslims continues, they will outnumber U.S. Jews before the decade ends.[16]

What this may bode for United States domestic affairs and foreign policy remains to be seen.

Central Americans

During the 1980s, the U.S. admitted hundreds of thousands of Central Americans. Although most begged for asylum, when political conditions improved, hardly any have been willing to return home.

Following the defeat of the Sandinistas, the new Vice President of Nicaragua, Virgilio Godoy, was met with a chorus of boos when he called on the self-exiled residents of Miami's "Little Managua" to go home and help reconstruct their native land. Said Miami-based Nicaraguan community leader Cristobal Mendoza, "He did not foresee what the reaction would be. It was shameful. How could this man come and say we should return?"[17]

On January 16, 1992, El Salvador's president and the guerrilla leaders signed a peace treaty, officially ending that over-populated country's 12-year-old civil war. An estimated 800,000 of El Salvador's 5.4 million people are already residing in the U.S., with 350,000 of them enjoying Congressionally-mandated "Temporary Protected Status" (TPS).

Few are eager to leave. Representative Joe Moakley (D-Mass) has sponsored legislation to extend TPS. Faced with the apparently unwelcome end (from their perspective) to their civil war, Salvadorans residing in the U.S. formed the Salvadoran National Network to lobby for an extension of TPS and to inform aliens of their rights. Network director Boris Canjura argues: "We believe the U.S. should help us rebuild our country, which means letting us stay here."[18]

Haitians

Thousands of Haitians are pleading to be admitted as refugees. Around one-sixth of the 6.3 million citizens of that poorest of Caribbean nations *already* reside in the United States.

If Haitians were genuine refugees — people fearing political persecution — we would expect them to be seeking sanctuary in the lands closest to their country. They could simply walk into the Dominican Republic, the neighboring portion of the island of Hispaniola, or they could flee to Cuba, 70 miles from Haiti. The Bahamas and Jamaica are just 100 miles away. Instead, they are heading to the U.S. — a hazardous 500 miles away.

A number of bills have been introduced in Congress to grant Haitians TPS. But most would likely end up staying permanently, as seems to be the case with Central Americans.

The Cuban Special Preference

Fidel Castro has been using emigration as a "safety valve" to get rid of Cuba's political dissidents, criminals, medical problems, and surplus population.

The Cuban Adjustment Act of 1966, a Cold War relic, grants Cuban nationals who reach the U.S. a number of special privileges, chief among them automatic permanent resident status after one year in the U.S.

The end of subsidies from the former Soviet Bloc has increased the economic stress on the once-prosperous island of Cuba. In an effort to stem reformist pressures, Castro has lowered the age requirements for travel abroad from 60 to 20, and encouraged youthful dissidents to depart. Many are taking advantage of this opportunity, rather than staying to fight for change.

And Now, Tibetans

The land-locked, mountainous country of Tibet was seized by China in 1950. Over the years, many Tibetans settled in Nepal and India. Today, 2.1 million live in Tibet proper, while over 4 million live in neighboring countries.

In 1993 the first group of Tibetans arrived in the U.S. Sponsored by the recently founded Tibet-U.S. Resettlement Project, they regard themselves as "the advance guard."

Dhondup Gonsar, executive director of the Tibetan Resettlement Project-Chicago, explained that they are afraid that the Chinese may eradicate Tibetan culture, and so they consider it "vitally important" to try to resettle in the U.S. and "preserve traditions and language."[19]

"Culture" Refugees

Political asylum has now been extended to include homosexuals and people claiming they are against their native land's traditions.

In the first case, on March 18, 1994, the Clinton Administration ordered the INS to grant asylum to an illegal alien from Mexico, who claimed that, as a practicing homosexual, he would be "persecuted" were he forced to go home. Jose Garcia has been in the U.S. illegally for a decade. At a deportation hearing in San Francisco, he complained that the Mexican police sometimes arrest patrons of homosexual bars and discourage them from loitering and engaging in sexual activity in public parks. The Mexican government vigorously denies that it oppresses homosexuals, though many Mexicans do not view it as a valid alternative lifestyle. This is the first time asylum has been given on such a basis. Said INS press aide, Duke Austin, "if a gay who's being persecuted in Mexico can get [asylum] on that grounds, then a gay who's been persecuted in any other country can get it on that grounds." If this decision stands, the U.S. will find itself the destination for millions of homosexuals, for there are few societies that consider homosexuals to be an "oppressed class" who merit special protection.[20]

In the second instance, a Nigerian citizen, Lydia Oluloro, was granted asylum by a judge in Oregon after she said her two daughters would likely be subjected to the African tribal custom of female circumcision. The practice is widespread throughout Africa, but is not forced upon females by the Nigerian government. Ms. Oluloro admitted that her own relatives would be the ones encouraging her daughters to undergo the operation. Again, if this decision is not overturned, half of Africa might claim asylum.[21]

Needed: A New Approach to Refugee Problems

The hard reality of surging Third World populations, political repression, and poverty, and the virtual absence of any countries willing to permanently resettle substantial numbers of refugees — especially economic ones — dictates the need for a whole new approach to refugee problems.

Genuine refugees are supposed to be individuals "who are in immediate danger of loss of life and for whom there appears to be no alternative to resettlement in the United States." Clearly, by this standard, relatively few of the hundreds of thousands of people admitted as "refugees" over the past twenty years actually qualify. "Refugee admission to a large degree is simply immigration by another name," Don Barnett points out, "where costs, normally incumbent upon the immigrant and his sponsor, have been shifted to the U.S. taxpayer."[22]

Moving a relatively few of the world's less fortunate to this country may salve the conscience of some involved in refugee services. But it fails to address the underlying demographic, political, and economic causes that foster the desire to emigrate. Our recommendations for a new approach are in Chapter Eleven.

Paradoxically, those who leave are most often the very people who best understand the language, culture, political, and economic systems of their home countries and are best qualified to help resolve the problems.

CHAPTER NINE
LOBBYING FOR OPEN BORDERS
THE PRO-IMMIGRATION COALITION

Since the early 1980s, public opinion polls have consistently shown that Americans want to reduce legal immigration and stop illegal immigration.

A 1990 poll revealed that, among U.S. citizens, 74 percent of whites and 75 percent of Mexican-Americans agreed that, "There are too many immigrants." A Roper poll conducted that same year revealed that 78 percent of black Americans oppose more immigration.[1]

And in spite of 1992 pre-election polls indicating that likely voters would favor candidates who supported immigration control, Bill Clinton, George Bush, and Ross Perot did not mention the issue during the presidential campaign. But the public has not forgotten this matter. Seventy-one percent of those responding to a Wall Street Journal/NBC poll released six weeks after the November election agreed that immigration should be cut back.[2]

A poll conducted by University of Texas professor Rodolfo de la Garza, the Latino National Political Survey, found that 80 percent of Puerto Rican Americans, 75 percent of Mexican-Americans, and 66 percent of Cuban-Americans want immigration to the U.S. reduced. The survey, released December 15, 1992, indicated that Latino concerns over immigration have actually grown over the past decade. These findings should help put to rest the notion that supporters of immigration restriction are xenophobes or worse.[3]

At least two major reasons explain this sustained concern. First, the prospect of millions of "would-be immigrants" flooding into this country from around the globe troubles most citizens. (Within hours of Bill Clinton's election, Haitians started building boats to set sail for the American land of milk and honey.)

Second, the American economy is undergoing fundamental restructuring, marked by dramatic downsizing. Over the past decade hundreds of thousands of blue-collar manufacturing jobs have been lost as have tens of thousands of professional positions. This trend will probably accelerate as the North American Free Trade Agreement (NAFTA) takes effect. Most people agree we simply do not need additional foreign job seekers.

Yet in spite of wide-spread public support for reducing immigration, in 1990 Congress increased legal immigration by 40 percent. And while the U.S. armed forces are deployed overseas to secure the borders of countries in the Far East, Middle East, and the Balkans, no similar effort has been made to secure our own borders against illegal trespass.

Public sentiment in favor of immigration control has not yet been translated into public policy, thanks to the efforts of a curious coalition of special interests. Who are those who favor virtually "open borders?"

Business Interests

Chief among them are Western agricultural interests, who want an endless supply of cheap, exploitable, compliant foreign labor. Agribusiness will do anything to retain its immigrant labor force, short of paying fair wages and providing tolerable living and working conditions. The social costs for immigrant workers, such as those for education, medical care, and subsidized housing, are simply passed along to the tax-paying public.

Big business has tended to be hostile to immigration reform. In late 1992, Walter Wriston, former chairman of

Citibank, argued for increased immigration on the TV program, "Wall Street Week." The editors of *The Wall Street Journal* have long called for a constitutional amendment that would simply state, "There shall be open borders."[4]

The "Open Borders" and "Free Trade" slogans have been used to help keep downward pressure on labor costs. And the threat of moving operations across the border has enabled some major firms to win wage and benefit concessions from their remaining American workers.

Foreign Capital

Aside from those who support open immigration for strictly philosophical reasons, there is a more sinister aspect to the immigration debate. In what the late President Richard Nixon had termed "a brilliant analysis," Professor Paul Gottfried points out in his new book, *The Conservative Movement*, that the Heritage Foundation, a Washington, D.C., think tank that has long influenced Republican policy makers, has received important financial support from Far Eastern governments and businessmen. Dr. Gottfried cites *National Journal* correspondent Dick Kirchten's observation that "immigration is a growth industry in the think tanks of the Right."

Heritage has aggressively promoted 'free trade' and increased Third World immigration to the U.S. It joined with Hispanic activists in opposing the employer sanctions provisions of the Immigration Reform and Control Act of 1986 (IRCA).[5]

Ethnic Politicians

Politicians, especially Democrats identified with Jesse Jackson's "Rainbow Coalition," see immigrants as a source of new voters and hence additional political power for themselves.

They support "same day," mail-in, and motor-voter registration that makes it all but impossible to verify that registrants are really citizens and entitled to vote.

The Clinton Administration has launched a special initiative to "actively encourage" amnestied illegal aliens and resident aliens to apply for citizenship and register to vote. INS Commissioner Doris Meissner has promised to take steps to "simplify" the naturalization process. These newly-recruited citizens will not only be able to vote, but will also have the right to bring in their immediate relatives as legal immigrants. Pro-immigration groups, such as Hermandad Mexicana Nacional (the National Mexican Brotherhood), have endorsed this campaign and are conducting their own "citizenship" classes for amnestied illegals and other aliens.

A number of self-appointed ethnic "leaders" see new waves of immigrants adding to their political support base. Although immigration restriction is endorsed by the vast majority of Hispanic Americans, this has not discouraged such organizations as the League of United Latin-American Citizens (LULAC), the Mexican-American Legal Defense and Education Fund (MALDEF), the National Council of La Raza (The Race), and National Immigration, Refugee and Citizenship Forum (NIRCF) from opposing immigration reform efforts.

Foundations

While the above groups clearly do not speak for rank and file Latino Americans, they do enjoy very generous funding from the Ford Foundation, which gave the four groups $31,082,672 from 1968 to 1992.[6] Other foundations and corporate institutions contributed additional millions. Financial statements reveal that nearly 100 percent of LULAC's budget derives from foundation and corporate donors, as does 93 percent of MALDEF's. These organizations have virtually no grassroots financial support.

Immigration Lawyers

Immigration to this country has become a growth industry for the legal profession. The 2000-plus members of the American Immigration Lawyers Association profit handsomely from the business generated by clients involved in lengthy refugee, asylum, residence, and assorted criminal alien cases. Often the lawyers' fees end up being paid by the government.

Government and Church Bureaucrats

Welfare agency bureaucrats welcome the influx of aliens. The social problems they generate need solutions! This leads to bigger budgets, and, as we have seen, immigration policies have been adding tens of thousands of individuals to the welfare rolls, while increasing the demand for other expensive social services, especially in education, health, and criminal justice.

Demetrios Papademetriou, head of the Carnegie Endowment's Immigration Policy Program, confirms this. He writes that immigration creates jobs for U.S. workers (to provide immigrants with government services), jobs for fellow nationals in immigrant enclaves, and an overall increase in jobs to provide the housing and other services immigrants consume.[7] Papademetriou is himself a prime example of those who owe their jobs to immigration, and who have an economic stake in keeping it going.

Refugee resettlement is big business. According to the State Department, organizations involved in refugee assistance receive a minimum of $588 from the federal government for each case they administer. Migration and Refugee Services, an arm of the U.S. Catholic Conference, is the largest refugee resettlement agency, handling nearly 40 percent of the annual refugee cases in the U.S.

The next largest resettlement agency is the New York-based Hebrew Immigrant Aid Society, which works primarily with Jews moving here from the former Soviet Union. Lutheran Immigration and Refugee Service and the Church World Service of the National Council of Churches are other major refugee resettlement agencies. Together, they constitute a very vocal and powerful lobby, with jobs of their own to protect.[8]

Some of the religious groups that oppose efforts to moderate and control population growth overseas, also advocate "Open Borders." Presumably the first stance required the second — the surplus people have to go somewhere.

Additionally, as active church membership has waned among some segments of American society, a number of religious leaders — Catholic, Protestant, Jewish, and Muslim alike — have come to view immigrants as a welcome source of new members. Jesuit Father Richard Ryscavage, executive director of Migration and Refugee Services, boasted that immigration "is the growing edge of Catholicism in the United States," and that the influx of 10 million immigrants since 1980 "is the key to our future."[9]

Political Idealogues

On the Left, some ideological critics of domestic and foreign policies view opposition to immigration control as one of the "fronts" on which "American imperialism" can be fought. For instance, the so-called "Sanctuary Movement," made up of people opposed to U.S. policy in Latin America, brought in people from the countries involved as a way to confront our government.

The National Lawyers Guild (NLG) is at the forefront of the campaign for virtually unrestricted immigration. Cited by Congress as the legal arm of the U.S. Communist Party, the collapse of the USSR has not led to its demise. The principle vehicle for NLG's activity in the field of immigration law and policy is its National Immigration Project, through which it continually whittles away in the courts at our immigration laws.

The American Civil Liberties Union (ACLU) is strongly opposed to any meaningful immigration reforms. ACLU executive director Ira Glasser has announced that their main objective is repeal of the employer sanctions provisions of the 1986 IRCA and opposition to a tamper-resistant identification system, such as Social Security cards, which would deter document fraud by illegal aliens and others.

The common thread running through all these refugee, church and other group efforts is a narrow, legalistic "rights" perspective — where civil rights are equated with "group rights." And "group rights" have spawned "immigrant rights" — which in turn have led to calls for "language rights." Environmental, economic and social cohesion concerns are all lost on these people.

Senator Edward Kennedy

No roster of the opponents of immigration reform would be complete without mentioning the special role played by Senator Edward Kennedy from Massachusetts. He was floor manager of the disastrous 1965 Immigration Bill. While urging its passage, he assured critics:

> *What the bill will not do: First, our cities will not be flooded with a million immigrants annually. Under the proposed bill, the present level of immigration remains substantially the same. ... Secondly, the ethnic mix of the country will not be upset. ... Contrary to the charges in some quarters, [the bill] will not inundate America with immigrants from any one country or area, or the most populated and economically deprived nations of Africa and Asia. ...*[10]

Senator Kennedy has long been chairman of the powerful Immigration Subcommittee of the Senate Judiciary Committee which considers all immigration legislation. Nothing passes without his approval. Only in 1986, when the Republicans temporarily enjoyed a majority in the Senate, did employer sanctions pass.

There can be little doubt that Senator Kennedy's opposition to immigration reform carries more weight than all the other factors listed here taken together. Should the voters of Massachusetts decide not to return him to office in the fall 1994 elections, the effect on immigration reform would be electric.

In Summary

Well-funded special interest groups have thus far thwarted the will of the American majority in the area of immigration reform: to end illegal immigration and substantially reduce legal immigration.

The success of these special interests highlights the need for concerned citizens to join together to support strong immigration control measures. These are outlined in Chapter Eleven.

PART THREE: THE SOLUTIONS

CHAPTER TEN
ETHICS AND MORALS: WHAT IS
THE RIGHT THING TO DO?

Many good-hearted and sensitive people who will have agreed with much of what we have written so far will still recoil from taking the actions necessary to remedy the immigration-related challenges we face. In a country with immigrant roots, this is understandable. If our forefathers had not migrated, where would we be now? Should not others have the same opportunity? After all, we have so much, and they have so little. Are we not just being selfish?

Then there is the Statue of Liberty, Emma Lazarus and her poem, all those immigrant Nobel Prize winners, and the wonderful rags-to-riches immigrant success stories.

So before we look at possible solutions to our immigration policy dilemmas, let us take time to formulate a basic set of ethical principles that can guide our thinking and decision making. Here are our suggestions for an immigration "Code of Conduct." We mention these particular principles because our opposition, in the main, holds contrary views.

A New Decalogue for an Increasingly Crowded World

Principle I: **World population growth** of 10,000 per hour, 250,000 per day, 90-plus million per year, dwarfs the absorptive capacity of the few countries still willing to receive legal (and certainly illegal) immigrants. The stresses caused by population growth cannot be solved by international migration. They must be confronted by and within each individual nation.

Principle II: The **nation-state**, remains an **essential** unit of human governance. Sovereignty is the guarantee of a nation's and its citizens' right to exist. Sovereignty includes the right to regulate entry into one's territory. The United Nations' *Universal Declaration of Human Rights*[1] recognizes this by enumerating a right of emigration, but not of immigration. The alternative to delineating and controlling borders is anarchy.[2]

Principle III: **Each nation** has a solemn **responsibility** to provide for the health, education, employment, and security of its own citizens. No nation can expect to solve deficiencies in these areas by exporting its surplus people. Fundamental to the concept of national rights and responsibilities is the duty of each nation to match its population with its political, social, and environmental resources, in both the short and the long term. No nation should exceed what the biologists call its "carrying capacity."

Principle IV: In setting its immigration policy, any nation must **first** look after the **interests of its own citizens**, including those at the bottom of the socio-economic ladder. The long term consequences of any actions, including the need to ensure social cohesion, and the long range management of social, political, and environmental resources must be considered. Passing these on in healthy condition to future generations must be a fundamental objective of public policy. This is not selfish; it is a requirement of social responsibility.

Principle V: **Each nation** should **train** its own technical and professional personnel, matching supply to demand. The developed countries in particular should not continue to encourage a brain drain from the less-developed countries, luring their talented people, and thus benefitting from the scarce capital that went into their education. On their part, the less-developed countries should educate their citizens in fields appropriate to their own country's needs, and not for some personnel export market.

Principle VI: **Each nation** should arrange to **do its own drudgery**, even if this means extra expense to improve the wages and conditions of service workers. Communities within the developed countries that have few or no immigrants have long demonstrated their ability to maintain themselves without outside help. In the long course of human history, there have always been those who wanted to harvest the product of another's labor. This was the underlying theme of slavery. It is time we closed this chapter of human history.

Principle VII: **Illegal immigration** is unacceptable, both for the individual migrant and for the recipient nation. Newcomers should arrive legally, indicating their respect for the laws and customs of their prospective new land. If workers have legal status, it will reduce the temptation of potential employers and others to exploit newcomers because of their illegal status. Illegal immigration should be held to the irreducible minimum.

Principle VIII: **Legal immigration** should come under the discipline of a "budget" concept, one that specifies an all-inclusive ceiling. If more in one category are to be admitted, balancing cuts must be made elsewhere.

The three fundamental questions that must be answered to set a policy on legal immigration are:

1. **How many** people shall we admit, and **what factors** should be taken into account in setting this limit?
2. **Who** should be chosen to immigrate, and **what criteria** should be used for choosing among candidates?
3. **How** can we humanely enforce the rules we decide upon?

To be taken seriously, any proposed legal immigration policy must set out specific answers to this "How-Who-How" trilogy.

To underscore the value of citizenship, legal immigrants should enjoy a lesser "bundle of rights" than citizens during their trial period of legal resident alien status. When they become eligible for naturalization, they should either commit themselves fully to their new country by becoming citizens and receiving full rights and accepting full responsibilities — or, if they choose not to make this commitment, should return home, making room for someone else. Both dual citizenship and permanent, lifelong resident alien status are ethically unacceptable. People should commit themselves to one polity or another, and participate fully in efforts to improve its social, political and economic life.

Principle IX: Concerning **asylees** and **refugees**, the emphasis should be on *temporary* succor with eventual repatriation, rather than permanent settlement. The UN High Commissioner for Refugees states that repatriation must be the solution for most refugee problems, given the numbers involved.[3] The limited refugee funds available are better spent on the relatively inexpensive per capita maintenance of many refugees in their region of origin, rather than on expensive permanent resettlement of a few in the developed countries. Refugees should not be introduced to the developed countries if there is to be any hope of repatriation.

Principle X: The **Epoch of International Migration** as a solution to human problems **is over** for the overwhelming majority of mankind. Most people will never be able to move from their place of birth — there are simply too many people and too few places left to go. Instead, individuals will have to work to change conditions they find unacceptable.

Many axioms and corollaries to this basic set of ten principles could and need to be enunciated. We believe, however, that these broad principles provide an overall framework for policy making. To these must be added a statement of the purpose of immigration, a concept with which we open the next chapter.

Postscript

The astute reader will note that we have not placed heavy emphasis on a plethora of "immigrants' rights," as is the inclination of the open borders lobby. Rather, we emphasize the rights (and responsibilities) of the citizens of the recipient countries.

In retrospect, surely no one should have expected that massive international migration could continue forever.[4] Times and our circumstances have changed since Emma Lazarus' sonnet was affixed to the Statue of Liberty in 1903.[5] Abraham Lincoln had the right perspective:

> *As our case is new, so we must think anew and act anew. We must disenthrall ourselves, and then we shall save our country.*[6]

CHAPTER ELEVEN
WHAT IS TO BE DONE? AN IMMIGRATION
POLICY FOR THE 21st CENTURY

There are three main aspects to our nation's immigration problem: illegal immigration, legal immigration, and asylees/refugees. Each of these requires separate attention and reform.

First, A Moratorium

Developing the political consensus needed for meaningful reforms will require time. Unfortunately, we do not have much time left. That is why the authors, with their combined 50 years of study of U.S. immigration problems, have concluded that first we need to declare an immediate moratorium on immigration into the U.S. — to enable us get the situation under control.

Only with a pause in immigration — a timeout — will we be able to coolly debate this issue, formulate strategies and implement new policies.

Throughout our history, periods of high immigration have always been followed by long breaks in the flow that provided time to assimilate recent arrivals. Such pauses in immigration occurred during the Colonial period, again through the 1860s and 1870s, and most recently from 1925 to 1965.

Since the mid-1960s, we have experienced nearly thirty years of massive, constantly expanding and uninterrupted immigration — greater than the heavy immigration between 1890 and 1914. In the last decade alone, the U.S. admitted nearly ten million legal immigrants. We believe that all the facts presented in this book provide ample evidence of the need for a hiatus, a breather, a "seventh immigration stretch" to assimilate the newcomers, to try to resolve the problems that have been created, and to consider what immigration policy we want for the future.

The first two of the earlier breaks mentioned above were *not* brought about as acts of deliberate public policy. They were accidents of history. However, the third one, beginning in 1917, was passed by Congress in response to popular demand.

As we related in Chapter Six, by 1924 Congress had passed laws reducing immigration from over 1 million a year down to about 150,000. This is what needs to happen again. And it is for this type of moratorium that we specifically call — with a reduction on the same order of magnitude.

If we limited immigration to only spouses and dependent, minor, never-married children of U.S. citizens, and a few bona fide political refugees, we would still be admitting about 200,000 persons per year … not as steep a cut as 1924.

As for refugees, the United States has done more than its fair share over the past fifty years, taking in more refugees for *permanent* resettlement than the rest of the world combined. (Many other countries take in people *temporarily*, until they can move on to some other country — too often the U.S.!) During the moratorium, we should call on the other signers of the UN Resolution on the Status of Refugees to do their part. Strictly acting as a *temporary* haven (for details, see the section below on asylum and refugees), the United States might continue to accept a very small number of refugees.

A moratorium would give us a chance to gain control of immigration and to have the open and honest public policy debate needed to frame the type of immigration policy we want for the 21st century.

What Is the Purpose of Immigration?

First and foremost, Congress must decide on the purposes of immigration, to guide its legislative efforts. Father Hesburgh and the Select Commission on Immigration & Refugee Policy called for this in the early 1980s. Amazingly, we still do not now have such a document or consensus on exactly what we are trying to achieve. It is little wonder then that we have an inconsistent and incoherent policy, since we do not know what our objectives are.[1]

In our view, such a statement would, as a minimum, make it clear that immigration is to serve, first and foremost, the interests of the American people. It should be subservient to other American goals for the general economy, employment, education, health, welfare, population and the environment. It would hold that illegal immigration is unacceptable and must be reduced to the practicable minimum. Finally, it would assert that We, the People (not previous immigrants nor others overseas), should determine who enters, in what numbers, and what measures will be used to enforce these limits.

Here are our ideas for a new immigration policy:

I. ILLEGAL IMMIGRATION

We consider illegal immigration first. If people are not following the rules governing entry into a country, it makes little difference what those rules are. So initially we must get illegal immigration under control.

Illegal aliens enter in one of two ways: they either enter the country by stealth without valid documents, or they come with legal documents, and then overstay their welcome. People cross into the United States chiefly over our land borders with Mexico and Canada, or through our ports — the air terminals and seaports.

The land border has two parts to it: the formal ports of entry, manned by the Customs and Immigration Services, where people can pass through legally and under inspection. Then there are the stretches between these entrances where *no one* is supposed to cross into this country. These are guarded by the U.S. Border Patrol, which had 4,000 agents at the end of 1993.

Immigration enforcement for the interior of the United States is the responsibility of the INS Investigations Division. With only 1,650 employees, called "special agents," the Investigations Division is the only INS law enforcement presence in our huge interior, non-border areas, and in urban centers, such as New York, Boston, Baltimore, Washington, D.C., Atlanta, St. Louis, and Chicago. Every year INS Investigators must contend with the 2 million or more aliens who manage to elude the Border Patrol, or who enter through our seaports and air terminals, often sporting tourist or student visas, or claim to be refugees seeking asylum. For this huge task, their ranks are thin indeed.

Protecting Our Border

To better prevent surreptitious entry across the border between the ports of entry, we need more Border Patrol agents and equipment; better barriers, including ditches and fences; better cooperation between the INS, the Customs Service and the Drug Enforcement Administration; use of the National Guard when appropriate; and access to military equipment as needed. We may very well need to deploy National Guard and regular military personnel on the border. Mexico and Israel do, as a way to control the illegal influx of people into their countries.

In February, 1982, Mexico created a 4,000-man quick reaction force to protect its own southern borders from aliens. The purpose of the force, according to a government spokesman, was "to defend the country's southern border ... against a spill-over of Central America's turbulent guerrilla wars."

A realistic goal for border enforcement measures is not absolute, 100 percent, prevention of illegal entry. Rather, as with any law enforcement issue, it is reducing it to tolerable levels.

It is simply not true that "we cannot" do much more to control our borders than we have in the past, as apologists for the status quo often argue. While U.S. armed forces are currently deployed around the globe to secure the borders of such distant countries as South Korea, Kuwait, and Macedonia (to name but a few), the fact remains that our political leaders have never tried to secure the borders of our country.

That securing our land borders is not an impossible task was demonstrated last fall when the El Paso, Texas, sector chief, Silvester Reyes, initiated "Operation Blockade." With an end-of- the-year grant of only $300,000 to provide overtime pay for 400 agents, Reyes deployed the Border Patrol 24-hours a day along the most frequently crossed stretch of the Rio Grande between Mexico and the United States. Illegal entry came to a virtual halt. Arrests of illegal aliens plunged from over 1,000 a day to an average of 135. It quickly became clear that one could no longer simply walk into the U.S.

The crackdown drew overwhelming support from the citizens of El Paso. Mayor Larry Francis exclaimed, "The rampant criminal problems in our downtown are gone. The majority of El Pasoans are stating that this should have been done long ago." The prostitutes who regularly congregated near City Hall disappeared. "I walked through downtown and all the underworld was gone. Particularly the pickpockets and transvestites weren't there," Mayor Francis observed. Fred Morales, a community activist, reported: "The stabbings and shootings are down to zero. This is the best present we could ever get."[2]

Building better barriers and maintaining patrols around the clock along the most heavily crossed areas can clearly go a long way toward minimizing illegal entry.

Securing Our Points of Entry

To prevent illegal entry through the ports of entry, we also need more personnel and better equipment to speed and increase the accuracy of inspections. Border-crossing documents should be machine-readable; more drug-sniffing dogs would be helpful; and a program to discourage document fraud is essential. A border-crossing fee of $2 could help pay for these measures. This compares with a $10 entrance fee charged foreigners at our air and sea ports (except for entrants from Mexico and Canada). Nearly every other country charges border crossing fees of some sort to cover the cost of border inspections.

The murderer of two CIA officials at the agency's head-quarters in Langley, Virginia, most likely entered the U.S. on a forged Pakistani passport. (Trade in fake visas flourishes in Karachi and Quetta — his points of departure.) Two weeks after he arrived in this country, he claimed that his passport had been lost and another was issued. This is a common tactic used by persons travelling on forged documents and underscores the need for more secure identification documents.

Controlling our ports of entry is a task of mammoth proportions. In any given year, over 300,000,000 aliens enter the U.S.[3] If we misjudge just one percent of those applying for admission, it comes to 3,000,000 people per year! That alone is more than 10 times our proposed moratorium flow! Cross-border traffic itself may need to be reduced, though this flies in the face of the new North American Free Trade Agreement (NAFTA), which was adopted without specific provisions for controlling immigration. These will now have to be arranged after the fact.

Disincentives

In addition to securing our borders and ports, the campaign against illegal immigration must include employer sanctions — penalties against employers who knowing hire persons not lawfully in the country and entitled to work here.

Employer sanctions must be defended against continuing attacks in Congress and the courts, and strengthened by some form of electronic or call-in verification system, so that employers can easily and accurately tell whether a prospective employee is legally in the country. This could work similarly to the system used by merchants to verify credit cards.

Second, denying health and welfare benefits to those not legally in the country is a must if we are not to become the hospital and welfare agency for the world. These benefits attract people and the costs are prodigious, as shown in Chapter Two. This will also require some system of secure identification to confirm that applicants are qualified to receive benefits.

Third, we need enhanced measures to counter crime, including anti-smuggling, anti-fraud, and violent gang task forces; better drug enforcement; and proactive as well as reactive efforts to deal with alien crime syndicates or criminal organizations.

Overstays

The problem of overstays can be addressed through better screening by our State Department and consular officers overseas where visas are issued. We need to consider such devices as bonds to assure return, and/or non-refundable round-trip airline tickets. All documents should be machine-readable at the ports of entry. Records of those who do not leave the country on time should be turned over to the INS Investigations Division for follow up.

Interior Enforcement

For all kinds of illegal immigration we need a vigorous interior enforcement system to apprehend illegals once they are in the country. We cannot tolerate a situation in which you are "home free" if you manage to slip into the country. This means hiring more agents for interior work. We must also insist that state and local police and social service authorities cooperate with the INS. This is now prohibited by many local governments, as we detailed in Chapter One.

Illegals in jail should have deportation hearings while still in custody so they can be deported immediately when they have served their time. They should not be allowed back into society, as now often happens.

Many other measures are possible and necessary, but this short list will show that it is feasible to control illegal immigration if we have the will to do so.

II. LEGAL IMMIGRATION

The basic and most fundamental requirement for legal immigration is an overall, inclusive ceiling covering *all* classifications of entrants, including refugees and asylees.

How might we set the ceiling for the numbers to be admitted? It certainly cannot be on the basis of demand, for there are literally tens of millions, if not billions, of people who would come to the United States if they could.

How Many and Who?

Rather, a ceiling must be set in view of our own national interests. The chief consideration, in our opinion, should be the demographic future we desire for the United States. How big do we want our population to get? And how fast do we want to get there? Of what groups do we want our population composed, and in what proportion? We need, as a nation, to debate and settle these points during the moratorium we have proposed.

During the 1970s and 1980s, picking an immigration ceiling was an easier proposition, since fertility in the U.S. was below replacement. We could afford some additions to our numbers through immigration and still look forward to stabilizing our population.

But now, in the 1990s, the U.S. fertility rate has gone back up to replacement level, an average of 2.1 children per couple. When population growth from immigration is added to this, it means that, if continued, the U.S. population will **never stop growing.**

We believe, as poll results suggest, that very few Americans want this. After all, our population has multiplied sixty-four times since four million people were counted in the first census in 1790; if it doubled two more times, we would be bigger than present-day India, nearly as large as China, with a standard of living headed in their direction.

If overall U.S. fertility rates rise above replacement, then immigration must virtually cease if we are to stabilize our population. Were this achieved, our population would continue to grow unless birthrates fell to replacement levels. Paradoxically, the main reason the U.S. birthrate has gone up is the high birthrates of recent immigrants.[4]

Three-hundred Million Is Enough!

Given current fertility rates, immigration must be sharply reduced if we Americans want to stabilize our numbers at 300 million — 20 percent above the 1990 level of 250 million. Three-hundred million Americans would be more than enough to provide any economies of scale, and might — with good planning, and a good measure of luck! — still allow us and our children to enjoy a decent quality of life for many years to come.

The alternative of perpetual population growth, with all that it implies for our political system, the environment, and the quality of our lives, is simply not acceptable.

Some Other Specific Measures

There are many other details on legal immigration that need attention. After clearly stating the purposes of immigration policy, and setting an overall ceiling, we need to:

- Stop chain migration, where the admission of married sons and daughters or married brothers and sisters opens up the spouses' extended families to immigration. We should admit only nuclear family units: spouses of U.S. citizens and their dependent, minor, never-married children.

- End the absurdity of granting U.S. citizenship simply by virtue of being born on U.S. soil, even if the parents are illegal aliens. Scholarly opinion holds that this *does not* require a constitutional amendment.[5]

- Deter marriage fraud, whereby an alien obtains legal resident status through a sham marriage to a U.S. citizen.

- Require foreign students to return home after their training in the U.S.

- Implement the Systematic Alien Verification for Entitlement (SAVE) program nationwide, to reduce fraudulent immigrant claims on welfare.

- Tie our immigration program to the needs of our labor market to assure that newcomers do not displace our own people in the work force. Move the administration of immigration back to the Labor Department, where it was before Franklin Roosevelt transferred it to the Justice Department in the 1940s.

- Assure that aliens do not get the right to vote until they are naturalized, and that illegal aliens are not counted for representation in our legislative bodies.

- Prohibit affirmative action benefits for immigrants.

- Give credits for knowing English in the selection of immigrants, and require English language skills in the naturalization exams that are high enough so that newly naturalized citizens can vote in English. Then repeal the bilingual ballot section of the Voting Rights Act, and end other mandated bilingual programs in education and public services.

- Fully automate the INS, and simplify the immigration laws so they are no longer a lucrative field for lawyers; charge adequate fees to cover the services rendered; provide citizens legal standing to sue to enforce immigration laws, and provide for a "sunset" on the basic immigration law, so that Congress must reconsider and revise it every few years (as is done with other programs) to help it conform to prevailing economic, social, and political conditions.

- Transform the Social Security card into a fraud-resistant identification document for **all** entitlement programs. Do the same for state drivers licenses (as has already been done in California).

- Close the local government-sponsored centers that help place illegal aliens in jobs.

- Finally, grant no more amnesties!

This is only a partial listing of measures that need to be taken. But enactment of these proposals would go far to achieve our goal of controlling immigration. All we need is the will to act.

III. ASYLEES AND REFUGEES

The question of how to deal with asylees and refugees is one facing all developed countries. With population "push" pressures developing as we explained in Chapter Eight, and with so few legal immigration avenues open, prospective immigrants are abusing the asylum and refugee system as a means of entering developed countries, including the U.S.

Temporary Succor

First of all, we need to completely revise our refugee policy, changing it to one of *temporary* haven rather than permanent residence. All the beneficiaries should agree in advance to repatriation when conditions at home allow it. Then, we must insist that the other 126 nations who have signed the UN Resolution on the Status of Refugees take their proportionate share of refugees.

The UN High Commissioner for Refugees argues that the main solution for refugee problems worldwide must be repatriation, with financial support for the countries of first asylum (usually a neighboring country).

We, in the U.S., can get the most good from the limited dollars we have available for refugee assistance by spending them on refugees in their country of first asylum. This will allow us to help many more people than does the current policy of bringing a few persons here for very expensive permanent resettlement. Then we should use all of the diplomatic and economic pressure at our disposal to improve the demographic, political, and economic conditions in source countries, to reduce the push for immigration.

End the Brain Drain

One effective way we can help the countries of origin is by assuring that their educated classes do **not** emigrate to the

U.S., but rather stay home and work to change the conditions they find unsatisfactory. How else can conditions be improved and the pressure for migration be reduced?

It would be self-satisfying and politically expedient to call for large-scale foreign aid to the source countries, since so many "refugees" are in reality economic migrants. But fifty years of foreign aid efforts leave us still debating what measures are effective. And, in any event, our till is empty. We would be less than candid to suggest that the world's migration problems can be solved through more foreign aid.

IV. THE END OF THE AGE OF MIGRATION

From the dawn of human history, picking up and moving on has been a workable solution to many human problems. However, there are no longer any vacant, habitable regions to which one can run. Every liveable area is now occupied, if not to its absolute carrying capacity, at least to a level where few of the current residents will welcome any newcomers.

Of all the members of the United Nations, only a handful still take in any substantial numbers of legal immigrants, and it seems very likely that even these countries will in the near future conclude that they have reached their limit. What then?

Mass migration is no longer a solution to human problems. People will now have to stay in the land of their birth, and work to change the conditions they do not like. This is the effort that should be occupying our attention and efforts, not shuffling the deck chairs on our global Titanic.

International migration is yesterday's solution for yesterday's less-crowded world.

CHAPTER TWELVE
WHAT YOU CAN DO

We hope the preceding chapter, and indeed this whole book, has shown that while immigration reform is a very complex, involved, and difficult problem, it *can* be solved. However, it will be a rare individual who can have much influence working all alone. Most of us just do not have the time, energy, or resources.

Rather, we must team up with others, pool our resources, and all play a role. People can work on the part of the problem suited to their talents and inclinations. Here is what you can do:

Distribute Copies of This Book

Help engage **your** friends and associates by distributing copies of *The Immigration Invasion*. There are order forms at the back of the book.

The Right to Write

Immigration reform requires a lot of writing — letters to the editor [the most-read part of the newspaper]; letters of praise or complaint to journalists as the situation warrants, whether on radio, TV, or in print; and to our public officials to educate and bring them along. Their addresses can be obtained from your local public library.

But, Above All...

Press on. Nothing takes the place of persistence. Keep on reading, writing, and talking, and in the end, we can win this contest of wills, just as our side won in 1924.

ENDNOTES

CHAPTER ONE
HEALTH AND WELFARE COSTS FOR IMMIGRANTS

[1] See also George J. Borjas, "Tired, Poor, On Welfare," *National Review*, December 13, 1993, pp. 40-42.

[2] Norman Matloff, "Easy Money, Lost Traditions," *National Review*, February 21, 1994, pp. 46-47.

[3] Center for Immigration Studies, *Estimated Annual Costs of Major Federal and State Services to Illegal Aliens*.

[4] Roy Beck, "Immigration: No. 1 in U.S. Growth," *The Social Contract*, Winter 1991-92, Vol. II, No. 2, pp. 106-108.

[5] *Los Angeles Times*, June 23, 1990.

[6] "INS Press Statement," January 21, 1994.

[7] Open letter to the President from the Governor of the State of California, August 10, 1993.

[8] Donald Huddle, "The Net Costs of Immigration to California," Washington, D.C.: Carrying Capacity Network, November 4, 1993.

[9] Reuters Dispatch, "Florida Seeks Immigration Reform," *Chicago Tribune*, February 12, 1994.

[10] New York State Senate Committee on Cities, *Our Teeming Shore*, Senator Frank Padavan, Chairman, January 1994.

[11] Diana Jean Schemo, "In Recession, Illegal Aliens Find a Cold Reception on Long Island," *The New York Times*, February 14, 1992.

[12] Don Barnett, *National Review*, November 1, 1993, p. 53.

[13] Don Huddle, "The Costs of Immigration," Washington, D.C.: Carrying Capacity Network, July 20, 1993.

[14] Daniel James, *Illegal Immigration: An Unfolding Crisis* (Lanham, MD: University Press of America, 1991).

CHAPTER TWO
LABOR MARKET IMPACT
SHOULD WE IMPORT MORE WORKERS?

[1] Ben Wattenberg, "Deficit Solution: Import Taxpayers," *The New York Post*, October 9, 1990.

[2] Julian Simon, "More Immigration Can Cut the Deficit," *The New York Times*, May 10, 1990.

[3] Vernon M. Briggs, Jr., "The Changing Nature of the Work Force: The Influence of U.S. Immigration Policy," *Looking Ahead*, Vol. XII, No. 4, pp. 8-17.

[4] "Larger Immigration and Looser Job Markets: Unemployment Outlook in Major Immigrant Receiving Areas," Center for Immigration Studies *Backgrounder* (December 1990).

[5] Bureau of Labor Statistics, 1993.

[6] Donald Huddle, Arthur Corwin, and Gordon MacDonald, *Illegal Immigration: Job Displacement and Social Costs* (Monterey, VA: American Immigration Control Foundation, 1985).

[7] Donald Huddle, *Immigration, Jobs and Wages: The Misuses of Econometrics and Immigration* and *Jobs: The Process of Displacement* (Teaneck, NJ: Negative Population Growth, Inc., 1992).

[8] Philip Martin, *Illegal Immigration and the Colonization of the American Labor Market* (Washington, D.C.: Center for Immigration Studies, 1986).

[9] Donatella Lorch, "Ethnic Niches Creating Jobs That Fuel Immigrant Growth," *The New York Times*, January 12, 1992.

[10] "The Soviet Brain Drain Is the U.S. Brain Gain," *Business Week*, November 4, 1991, p. 94.

[11] Letter to Wayne Lutton from William Jones, Southwestern University, Georgetown, TX, May 11, 1992.

[12] Steve Johnson, "Stanford Offers Born-in-U.S. Minority Bonus," *San Jose Mercury News*, October 24, 1993.

[13] "An Immigrant-Worker Scheme Comes Under Fire," *Business Week*, November 8, 1993, p. 40.

[14] *Labor Law Journal*, August 1991.

[15] Michael Lind, "Immigration Epiphany" (letter to the editor), *National Review*, March 7, 1994, p.2.

**CHAPTER THREE
IMMIGRATION AND THE POLITICS
OF RACE, LANGUAGE, AND CULTURE**

[1] U.S. Immigration and Naturalization Service, *Statistical Yearbook of the Immigration and Naturalization Service, 1992* (U.S. Government Printing Office: Washington, D.C., 1993).

[2] Mark Shaffer, "Heated Language over Citizenship Rites," *The Arizona Republic*, July 1, 1993, pp. A-1 and A-10.

[3] From Registrar-Recorder/County Clerk, Los Angeles, CA, 1992.

[4] Jim Keary, "Foreign Residents Vote for First Time in Takoma Park," *The Washington Times*, November 2, 1993, p. C-9.

[5] Paul Craig Roberts, "Government Stole Our Citizenship," *The Detroit News*, June 11, 1993, p. 11A.

[6] From Office of the Commissioner of Official Languages, Ottawa, Canada, March 3, 1994 (phone call).

[7] From Board of Education, Washington, D.C.

[8] "Public Service Commission Annual Report 1992," *APEC Newsletter* (Alliance for the Preservation of English in Canada), October 1993, Vol. XVI, No. 8.

[9] Philip L. Martin, "Migration and Trade: Challenges for the 1990s," from a paper presented at the World Bank, Washington, D.C., February 4, 1994.

CHAPTER FOUR
IMMIGRATION AND CRIME

[1]   Dianne Klein, "A Hit or Miss Approach to Curbing Deportable

Felons," *Los Angeles Times*, November 27, 1993; Joe Brogran, "Criminal Aliens Costly, Difficult to Deport," *Palm Beach Post*, February 23, 1992; Associated Press, "Rising Crime Among Aliens Puts Strain on Justice System in the U.S.," *The Washington Times*, November 27, 1989.

[2] Special Report, "Global Mafia," *Newsweek*, December 13, 1993.

[3] *U.S. News & World Report*, January 18, 1988.

[4] On the Chinese Triads, see Gerald Posner, *Warlords of Crime* (New York: McGraw-Hill, 1988); Martin Booth, *The Triads* (New York: St. Martin's Press, 1991); Gwen Kinkead, *Chinatown: Portrait of a Closed Society* (New York: Harper/Collins, 1992).

[5] U.S. General Accounting Office, *Nontraditional Organized Crime*, 1989, pp. 42-47.

[6] State of California, Department of Justice, *Organized Crime in California: Annual Report to the California Legislature*, State of California, Department of Justice, 1989 and following.

[7] David Kaplan and Alec Dubro, *Yakuza* (Reading, MA: Addison-Wesley, 1986); State of California, Department of Justice, *Organized Crime in California: Annual Report to the California Legislature*, State of California, Department of Justice, 1989 and following.

[8] *Business Week*, July 8, 1991, p. 29.

[9] George Volsky, "Jamaican Drug Gangs Thriving in Big U.S. Cities," *The New York Times*, July 19, 1987; Mary Thornton, "U.S. Rounding Up Jamaican Drug Gangs," *The Washington Post*, October 21, 1987; Sharon Cohen, Associated Press, "Jamaican Gangsters Building U.S. Empire," *Denver Post*, January 17, 1988; Eric Harison, "Drug-Dealing 'Posses' Jamaicans," *Los Angeles Times*, January 3, 1989; General Accounting Office, *Nontraditional Organized Crime*, 1989; Joe Brogan, "Agents Playing 'Cat and Mouse' With Jamaican Drug Dealers," *Palm Beach Post*, March 30, 1992.

[10] Stephen Handelman, "The Russian 'Mafia,'" *Foreign Affairs*, March/April 1994, pp. 83-96.

[11] Harry Seper, "The Russian Mafia," *Insight*, October 21, 1991, p. 18.

[12] Nathan Adams, "Menace of the Russian Mafia," *Reader's Digest*, August 1992, pp. 33-40; Craig Copetas and Chapin Wright, "Russian Mob Thrives in Brighton Beach," *New York Newsday*, September 21, 1992.

[13] "The Wise Guys of Russia," *U.S. News & World Report*, March 7, 1994, pp. 41-47.

[14] Peter Moses and Carl Pelleck, "Attack of the Kosher Nostra," *New York Post*, August 27, 1986; "Israeli Mafia Grows in U.S.," *The Jerusalem Post*, September 22, 1990.

[15] Associated Press, "Nigerian Jailed: Heroin Found in Typewriter," *Detroit Free Press*, March 11, 1990.

[16] Frank Wolfe, "Arlington Police Link Nigerians, Credit Card Fraud," *The Washington Times*, October 24, 1991; David Simcox, "The Nigerian Crime Network," *The Social Contract*, Spring 1993, Vol. III, No. 3, pp. 168-170; Frank Greve, "Americans Fall Victim to Foreign Con Artists: Scams from Nigeria Snare Several People Each Month," *Detroit Free Press*, September 27, 1993.

[17] *Criminal Aliens in the Los Angeles County Jail Population*, Final Report, November 1990, Office of Lieutenant Governor Leo MacCarthy.

[18] New York State Senate Committee on Cities, *Our Teeming Shores*, January 1994, pp. 24-36.

[19] Thomas Jackson, "Mexico Moves North," *American Renaissance*, Vol. 5, No. 1, January 1994, p. 8; *New York Times*, December 11, 1993; *Chicago Tribune*, December 12, 1993, Sec. 1, p. 30.

[20] "Violent Youth Gangs Frighten Los Angeles and Split the Races," *The New York Times*, February 8, 1988; General Accounting Office, *Nontraditional Organized Crime*, September 1989; James Dao, "Asian Street Gangs Emerging as Violent New Underworld," *The New York Times*, April 1, 1992; Conrad deFiebre, "Police in St. Paul Fear Rise in Crime Among Asian Youth," *Minneapolis Star Tribune*, Dec. 19, 1991; Kim Shuetz, "Violent Gangs are Growing Concern in Holland," *The Grand Rapids Press*, May 23, 1991; Lisa Perlman, "Youth Crime Takes the Bloom Off City Famed for Tulips," *Detroit News*, May 2, 1993.

[21] Elaine Shannon, *Desperados* (New York: Viking Press, 1989).

[22] Gus Tyler, "Poisoning the U.S. Market," *Forward*, February 4, 1994, p. 7.

[23] James M. O'Kane, *The Crooked Ladder* (New Brunswick: Transaction Publishers, 1992).

[24] See Dick Kirschten, "Tempest-Tossed Task," *Government Executive*, October 1993, pp. 34-38.

[25] Roberto Suro, "U.S. Halts Immigrant Fingerprint Checks," *The Washington Post*, April 14, 1994, p. 11.

CHAPTER FIVE
THE ENVIRONMENT AND QUALITY OF LIFE

[1] Roy Beck, "Immigration No. 1 in U.S. Growth," *The Social Contract*, Vol. II, No. 2, Winter 1991-92, p. 106.

[2] Gary Blonston, "Census Forecast for 2050 Gives Minorities Big Gains," *Detroit Free Press*, December 4, 1992, p. 3A.

[3] Tim Bovee, "Census Sees Radical Shifts in U.S. Racial, Ethnic Mix," *The Birmingham News*, September 29, 1993.

[4] From California State Driver Motor Vehicle records, February 28, 1994 (phone call).

[5] See in general Jack Parsons, *Population Versus Liberty* (London: Pemberton Books, 1971).

[6] Richard Lacayo, "The 'Cultural' Defense," *Time*, Fall 1993, p. 61.

[7] Edward Abbey, *Abbey's Road* (New York: E. P. Dutton, 1979), p. 137.

CHAPTER SIX
HOW DID WE GET INTO THIS PREDICAMENT?
A BRIEF HISTORY OF U.S. IMMIGRATION
CONTROL POLICIES THROUGH 1952

[1] For an explanation of how Emma Lazarus' poem was added to the Statue of Liberty, and how the symbolism of the statue has been

changed from its intended meaning, see Elizabeth Koed, "A Symbol Transformed: How 'Liberty Enlightening the World' Became 'The Mother of Exiles,'" *The Social Contract*, Vol. II, No. 3, Spring 1992, pp. 134-143.

[2] See James Clifton, ed., *The Invented Indian*, New Brunswick, New Jersey: Transaction Publishers, 1990; Roger Pearson, *Anthropological Glossary*, Malabar, Florida: Robert E. Krieger Publishing Co., 1985, p. 125.

[3] See Wayne Lutton, *The Myth of Open Borders: The American Tradition of Immigration Control* (Monterey, VA: American Immigration Control Foundation, 1988) for a review of immigration control efforts from Colonial times to 1965.

[4] The views of American statesmen on these issues have been compiled and are included in *The Founders of the Republic on Immigration, Naturalization and Aliens*, edited by Madison Grant and Charles Stewart Davison (New York: Charles Scribner's Sons, 1928; reprint, Washington, D.C.: Scott-Townsend Publishers, 1994).

[5] Booker T. Washington, "Education Before Equality: The Atlanta Exposition Address, 1895," from *Afro-American History: Primary Sources*, second edition, edited by Thomas R. Frazier (Chicago: Dorsey Press, 1988) pp. 193-196.

CHAPTER SEVEN
THE OPENING OF THE FLOODGATES
IMMIGRATION POLICY AFTER 1952

[1] David M. Reimers, "An Unintended Reform: The 1965 Immigration Act and Third World Immigration to the United States," *Journal of American Ethnic History*, Fall 1983, pp. 9-28.

[2] Lawrence Auster, *The Path to National Suicide*, cf. Chapter One, "The 1965 Act: Its Intent, Its Consequences" (Monterey, VA: American Immigration Control Foundation, 1990), p. 12.

[3] Peter Brimelow, "Time to Rethink Immigration?," *National Review*, June 22, 1992, pp. 30-46.

[4] Palmer Stacy and Wayne Lutton, *The Immigration Time Bomb*

(Monterey, VA: American Immigration Control Foundation, 1985), p. 20.

[5] "Rights Leader Charged in Immigration Fraud," *The New York Times*, April 7, 1994.

CHAPTER EIGHT
THE WORLD COMES TO THE U.S.

[1] Seth Mydans, "More Mexicans Come to U.S. to Stay," *The New York Times*, January 21, 1991; Tim Golden, "Mexicans Head North Despite Rules on Jobs," *The New York Times*, December 13, 1991.

[2] Lindsey Grant, "Missing Airline Passengers," *The Social Contract*, Summer 1993, Vol. III, No. 4, pp. 251-258.

[3] Matt Moffett, "Border Midwives Bring Baby Boom to South Texas," *The Wall Street Journal*, October 16, 1991.

[4] Tom Bethell, "Immigration: The Problem is Federal Rules," *Los Angeles Times*, September 12, 1993.

[5] Donald Huddle, "Immigration," *Chronicles*, March 1994, pp. 4-5.

[6] Peter H. Schuck and Rogers M. Smith, *Citizenship Without Consent* (New Haven: Yale University Press, 1985).

[7] All immigrant and refugee/asylee numbers are from the Department of Justice, Immigration & Naturalization Service.

[8] Adrian Karatnycky, "In Global Vacuum, Tyranny Advances," *The Wall Street Journal*, December 16, 1993.

[9] Don Barnett, "Free Pass to Disneyland: Soviet Emigres on the Dole," *Chronicles*, February 1992, pp. 41-44.

[10] Don Barnett, "Their Teeming Shores," *National Review*, November 1, 1993, pp. 51-55.

[11] Sarah Gauch, "Arab Americans Making Mark; Debate: Increase in Immigration Adds Steam to Issue of Minority Status," *The Detroit News*, February 13, 1994.

[12] Matthew Dorf, "Minority Status Eyed by Arabs," *Forward*, January 28, 1994.

[13] Tarek Hamada, "Chaldeans Eager for U.S. Homes," *The Detroit News*, June 18, 1993.

[14] Mary Hill, "Family Flees Strife in Somalia," *Chicago Tribune*, December 9, 1992.

[15] Lynne Duke, "Islam Is Growing in U.S., Despite an Uneasy Image," *The Washington Post*, October 24, 1993.

[16] R. Gustav Niebuhr, "American Moslems: Islam Is Growing Fast In the U.S.," *The Wall Street Journal*, May 10, 1990.

[17] Jorge Casuso, "Exiles face no-win decision," *Chicago Tribune*, March 1, 1990.

[18] Linda Feldmann, "Salvadoran Immigrants Feel Tense Uncertainty About Future Status," *The Christian Science Monitor*, January 30, 1992.

[19] Connie Lauerman, "Reasons to Celebrate," *Chicago Tribune*, February 24, 1993.

[20] "Gay Mexican given asylum for persecution," *The Washington Times*, March 26, 1994, p. A5.

[21] Editorial, "Redefining political asylum," *New York Post*, April 8, 1994.

[22] Don Barnett, *National Review*, November 1, 1993, p. 53.

CHAPTER NINE
LOBBYING FOR OPEN BORDERS
THE PRO-IMMIGRATION COALITION

[1] From the Roper Organization, "Summary of Key Findings 1990 National Roper Poll on Immigration," April 20-May 2, 1990.

[2] From The Wall Street Journal/NBC Poll, December 1992.

[3] Roberto Suro, "Hispanic Pragmatism Seen in Survey," *The New York Times*, December 15, 1992; Lynne Duke, "Poll of Latinos Counters Perception on Language, Immigration," *The Washington Post*,

December 16, 1992.

[4] Editorials, *The Wall Street Journal*, July 3, 1984, July 3, 1986, July 3, 1989.

[5] Paul Gottfried, *The Conservative Movement* (New York: Twayne/Macmillan, 1993), pp. 138-139.

[6] See the chart in *The Social Contract*, Volume IV, No. 3 (Spring 1994) p. 198, created from the Ford Foundation's Annual Reports showing the contributions to various lobbying groups over the past 25 years.

[7] Demetrios Papademetriou, "Immigration's Effects on the United States," *Interpreter Releases*, Vol. 71, No. 1, January 3, 1994.

[8] From the Office of Refugee Resettlement; Jewish Telegraphic Agency, October 1993.

[9] *National Catholic Register*, November 8, 1992.

[10] Lawrence Auster, *The Path to National Suicide*, cf. Chapter One, "The 1965 Act: Its Intent, Its Consequences" (Monterey, VA, American Immigration Control Foundation, 1990), p. 12.

CHAPTER TEN
ETHICS AND MORALS
WHAT IS THE RIGHT THING TO DO?

[1] *Universal Declaration of Human Rights*, December 10, 1948, Article 13, No. (2).

[2] Robert D. Kaplan, "The Coming Anarchy," *The Atlantic Monthly*, February 1994, pp. 44-76.

[3] See in general "The State of World Population 1993," United Nations Fund for Family Planning.

[4] See John Tanton, "End of the Migration Epoch?," *The Social Contract*, Spring 1994, Vol. IV, No. 3, pp. 162-176.

[5] See Elizabeth Koed, "A Symbol Transformed: How 'Liberty Enlightening the World' Became 'The Mother of Exiles,'" *The Social Contract*, Spring 1992, Vol. II. No. 3, pp. 134-143.

[6] Abraham Lincoln, "Second Annual Message to Congress," December 1, 1862; from John Bartlett, *Familiar Quotations, 15th Edition* (Little Brown and Company: Boston, 1980), p. 522, Item 12.

CHAPTER ELEVEN
WHAT IS TO BE DONE?
AN IMMIGRATION POLICY FOR THE 21st CENTURY

[1] For those who wish to pursue this topic, we recommend Otis L. Graham, Jr.'s *Rethinking the Purposes of Immigration Policy*, 1991 (Center for Immigration Studies, 1815 H Street, N.W., #1010, Washington, D.C. 20006, $6.95).

[2] Richard Woodbury, "Slamming the Door," *Time*, October 25, 1993, p. 34; John L. Martin, "Operation Blockade: A Bullying Tactic or a Border Control Model?," Center for Immigration Studies *Backgrounder* (December 1993).

[3] The most recent figures available are for 1992, when more than 314 million aliens were inspected at U.S. ports of entry. U.S. Immigration and Naturalization Service, *Statistical Yearbook of the Immigration and Naturalization Service, 1992* (Washington, D.C.: U.S. Government Printing Office, 1993), p. 170.

[4] Leon Bouvier, *Fifty Million Californians?* (Washington, D.C.: Center for Immigration Studies, 1991).

[5] Peter H. Schuck and Rogers M. Smith, *Citizenship Without Consent* (New Haven: Yale University Press, 1985).

Articles

Brimelow, Peter. "Time to Rethink Immigration?." *National Review* (June 22, 1992).

Davis, Kingsley. "The Migrations of Human Populations." *Scientific American* (September 1974).

Huddle, Donald. "Immigration, Jobs and Wages: The Misuses of Econometrics." *NPG Forum* (April 1992); "Immigration and Jobs: The Process of Displacement." *NPG Forum* (May 1992).

Miles, Jack. "Blacks vs. Browns." *The Atlantic Monthly* (October 1992).

Kaplan, Robert D. "The Coming Anarchy." *The Atlantic Monthly* (February 1994).

"Demystifying Multi-culturalism." *National Review* (February 21, 1994), pp. 26-54.

Beck, Roy. "The Ordeal of Immigration in Wausau." *The Atlantic Monthly* (April 1994).

Books and Monographs

Abernethy, Virginia. *Population Politics: The Choices That Shape Our Future*. New York: Plenum Publishing, 1993.

Auster, Lawrence. *The Path to National Suicide: An Essay on Immigration and Multiculturalism*. Monterey, VA: American Immigration Control Foundation, 1990.

Bouvier, Leon F. *Fifty Million Californians?*. Washington, D.C.: Center for Immigration Studies, 1991.

Bouvier, Leon F. *Peaceful Invasions: Immigration and Changing America*. Lanham, MD: University Press of America, 1991.

Grant, Lindsey (ed.). *Elephants in the Volkswagen: Facing the Tough Questions About Our Overcrowded Country*. New York: W. H. Freeman and Company, 1992.

Hardin, Garrett. *Living Within Limits*. New York: Oxford University Press, 1993.

Lutton, Wayne. *The Myth of Open Borders: The American Tradition of Immigration Control*. Monterey, VA: American Immigration Control Foundation, 1988.

Nelson, Brent. *America Balkanized*. Monterey, VA: American Immigration Control Foundation, 1994.

Schlesinger, Arthur M., Jr.,*The Disuniting of America*, New York: W. W. Norton, 1992.

You may wish to join some of these ...

ORGANIZATIONS WORKING ON IMMIGRATION POLICY

Membership Organizations

Federation for American
   Immigration Reform
   (FAIR)
1666 Connecticut Ave., NW
Suite 400
Washington, D.C. 20009
PHONE: (202) 879-3000
FAX: (202) 387-3447
Annual Membership: $25.00

English Language Advocates
P.O. Box 96481
Washington, D.C. 20077-7873
PHONE: (800) 773-2587
FAX: (616) 347-1185
Annual Membership: $20.00

Negative Population Growth,
   Inc. (NPG)
210 The Plaza — Box 1206
Teaneck, NJ 07666-1206
PHONE: (201) 837-3555
FAX: (201) 837-0288
Annual Membership: $30.00

Population-Environment
   Balance
1325 "G" Street, NW
Suite 1003
Washington, D.C. 20005-3104
PHONE: (202) 879-3000
FAX: (202) 879-3019
Annual Membership: $25.00

Carrying Capacity Network
1325 "G" Street, N.W., #1002
Washington, D.C. 20005
PHONE: (202) 879-3044
FAX: (202) 879-3019
Annual Membership: $20.00

Californians for Population
Stabilization (CAPS)
926 "J" St., Suite 915
Sacramento, CA 95814
PHONE: (916) 446-1033
FAX: (916) 446-7854
Annual Membership: $30.00

Sierra Club Population Comm.
408 "C" Street, N.E.
Washington, D.C. 20002
PHONE: (202) 547-1141
FAX: (202) 547-6009
Annual Membership: $35.00

Think Tank

Center for Immigration Studies
1815 H Street NW, Suite 1010
Washington, D.C. 20006
PHONE: (202) 466-8185
FAX: (202) 466-8076

Periodical

The Social Contract
316½ E. Mitchell St. #4
Petoskey, MI 49770
PHONE: (616) 347-1171
FAX: (616) 347-1185
Annual Subscription: $25.00

ORDER FORM

FOR ADDITIONAL COPIES OF
The Immigration Invasion

Name _____

Address _____

_____

City _____ State _____ Zip_____

(All prices include postage and handling)

- ☐ 1 copy $4.00
- ☐ 2-49 copies $2.00 each
- ☐ Case of 50 copies $55.00

Total number of copies ordered _____ = $_____

(Please makes checks payable to the Social Contract Press)

Mail this form to:

The Social Contract Press
316½ E. Mitchell St., Suite 4
Petoskey, MI 49770

We will be happy to send *The Immigration Invasion* directly
to your friends. Please enclose the name and address of the
person to receive the book as well as payment of $4.00 for
each name listed.

ABOUT THE AUTHORS

Wayne C. Lutton, Ph.D., is a policy analyst and an historian who has published widely on population and immigration concerns. A native of Illinois, he attended Bradley University (B.A., International Studies), Colorado College, University of South Carolina, and Southern Illinois University (Ph.D., History). Dr. Lutton was for five years research director for an educational institute and has been a college professor, teaching courses on the history and politics of Modern Europe, the United States, and Latin America. He has given a number of scholarly papers dealing with U.S.-Latin American relations and nationalist movements in the Third World. Dr. Lutton is currently associate editor of *The Social Contract*.

He is author, co-author, or contributor to ten books and monographs, including *The Immigration Time Bomb* (1985; revised edition, 1988) and *The Myth of Open Borders* (1988). Essays by him are published in *Immigration: Opposing Viewpoints* (1990), a college text, and in *Will America Drown? Immigration and the Third World Population Explosion* (1993). He has written nearly two-hundred articles and reviews which have appeared in *Chronicles*, *National Review*, *The Social Contract*, *Strategic Review*, and other journals of scholarship and opinion.

Dr. Lutton is a frequent guest on radio and television talk shows and has addressed audiences throughout the U.S., in Canada, and Great Britain.

John H. Tanton, M.D., is an eye surgeon who practices in the small town of Petoskey in northern Michigan.

An ardent conservationist since his farmboy youth, Tanton concluded as he was finishing medical school at the University of Michigan in 1960 that continued human population growth was a big part of the conservation problem. This conviction led him by turns to the chairmanship of the National Sierra Club Population Committee (1971-74), the national board of Zero Population Growth (1973-78), and its national presidency (1975-77). In 1979, as immigration grew to the point of becoming a population problem, he organized the Washington, D.C.-based Federation for American Immigration Reform (FAIR) to work on all aspects of U.S. immigration policy. He continues on the FAIR board, after serving as its chairman for the first eight years. He also helped organize and serves on the board of English Language Advocates (ELA), a group countering the growing language divisions in our society.

Dr. Tanton is author of *Rethinking Immigration Policy* and a contributor to *Alternatives to Growth: A Search for Sustainable Futures*. His articles on population, immigration, and related topics have appeared in *The Christian Science Monitor*, *The Ecologist*, and *The Houston Chronicle*. He is the editor and publisher of *The Social Contract*, a quarterly journal.